WORLD
TRAVELPASS
GUIDE
1991/92

Published by Thomas Cook Publishing
The Thomas Cook Group Ltd.
PO Box 227
Peterborough PE3 6SB
England.

ISBN 0 906273 03 X

Typesetting converted by Riverhead Typesetters Ltd., Grimsby.
Printed and bound in Great Britain by Albert Gait Ltd., Grimsby.

CONTENTS

EDITORIAL

From humble beginnings in 1987 (pilot issue) as a railpass guidebook the Thomas Cook Railpass Guide has progressed both in size - from an original 32 pages - and content to this year's World Travelpass Guide, containing not only a wealth of information on rail and road public transport offers worldwide but now including details of air travel passes. Regular users of the book will not need reminding that the "old faithfuls" such as InterRail Cards, Eurail Passes and rail passes in France, Germany, Italy, Netherlands, Scandinavia, Spain, the United Kingdom , the United States and many other countries are up-dated once again. But as well as these popular tried and tested passes and the many regional and city transport reduced-rate travel tickets which have adorned the guidebook in previous years we have added details of public transport passes in such diverse places as around Lake Balaton, in Salzburg, Prague, Blackpool, East Yorkshire, Edinburgh, Northern Scotland, North Wales and Essex, on Berchtesgadener Bergbahn services in Germany and on ships operating on Swiss Lakes, throughout the Western Isles of Scotland and among the Greek Islands. Together with information on air travel passes in nineteen countries we trust you will find the first edition of the Thomas Cook World Travelpass guide to be a truly helpful aid to what we hope is very pleasant (and reasonably cheap!) travelling by land, on water and in the air.

Symbols used in the guidebook:

☎ for telephone numbers

⛴ for shipping services by sea, on lakes and rivers

🚌 for bus/motor coaches services

🚃 for all rail services

✈ for air travel services

U for all forms of urban transport - usually bus, tram (trolley), Metro/Underground railways, urban/suburban railways; sometimes ferry services, cable cars, etc.

Thomas Cook through their United Kingdom general sales agents *Compass* represent overseas travel companies and market a number of their products. Those covered in this guidebook are Amtrak's USA Rail Passes, Via Rail's Canrailpasses and the Greyhound Canada Pass, Austrail and Budget Austrail Passes issued by Railways of Australia as well as the Kangaroo 'Road 'N Rail' Pass, InterCity Travelpasses in New Zealand, Japan Rail Passes and Greyhound Bus Passes in Australia and the USA. The general public may book these passes through Thomas Cook retail shops and those in the travel trade may reserve through Compass at PO Box 113, Peterborough PE1 1LE; ☎0733-51780; fax 0733-892601.

GENERAL NOTES

Air Travel Passes

Air travel passes are available in a number of forms, offering reductions on standard advertised fares by scheduled services. The most common variety is the pass issued with a series of coupons (usually a minimum of two) with each coupon valid for a sector of travel, for a particular flight journey or for one day's travel - which may involve a change of flights. Additional coupons may be purchased for further travel and children are required to have the same number of coupons as accompanying adults. The passes can be used in a country or in a continent (e.g. North America) on the scheduled services of a national carrier and their associate airlines with sometimes the stipulation that arrival in and departure from that country must be by international flights of the airline issuing the pass. Back-tracking along a route already travelled is not normally allowed unless it is necessary in order to make a connecting flight. Passes can often be purchased in advance together with round trip international flight tickets.. Restrictions are placed on the number of voluntary stopovers allowed though not on the amount of time spent at the stopover. Passes are available only to non-residents of countries where they are to be used. Yet another type of pass is one based on fixed itineraries where major cities and resorts can be visited once but only the international arrival and departure point can be visited more than once. There are reductions in some countries for air travel by senior citizens. Requirements for purchase of passes are proof of overseas residency and the holding of valid international return tickets.

Alterations to Information

Most public transport companies fix the prices and availability of their passes for the calendar year or for the duration of the main tourist season (in the northern hemisphere April/May to October). The fares and other details shown are the latest received but are subject to alteration and are given only as a guide, bearing in mind the number of factors which can cause prices and conditions to change. New offers are sometimes introduced during the year whilst price increases may be necessary due to economic pressures. Where prices for the current year are not known, the previous year's prices are quoted.

Bargains

The inclusion of a pass in this book is not meant to imply that it is necessarily the cheapest travel option for any given journey. Reduced-rate off-peak or excursion tickets may be available at lower prices on specific dates or days of the week but are usually advertised only in the area concerned. Special offers to students, senior citizens and groups (refer to the section headed "Groups") may often be available. But the Rover type of ticket offering ride-at-will travel with few, if any, restrictions give good value for money in their wide-ranging coverage.

Bus Passes

National, regional and city bus passes are now common in many countries and offer a cheap and independent way of getting to see as much of interest as possible. In the United Kingdom, Australia, New Zealand etc., long-distance buses are known as coach or motor coach services.

Change of Class

Rail pass holders wishing to travel in a higher class than that of their ticket should first contact the conductor as soon as possible and will then be required to pay only the difference between the ordinary lower and upper class fares for the journey being made. Failure to give prior notice of change of class can result in a fine. If time allows, excess tickets can usually be issued at a ticket office before commencement of the journey.

Children's Fares

The age limits and reductions for children are usually shown following the details of each adult ticket where known. A railpass covering travel in countries with differing child fare age limits will normally be valid only to the lowest of these limits.

City Transport Passes

Urban transport passes have been included on the basis of a pass covering all forms of city transport - buses/trams(trolleys), urban railways (including light railways), Metro/underground railways - though in a few cases city transport is by bus only. In some cities passes can be used on local ferry services, cable cars or funicular railways. In many cases, tickets have to be validated in machines on station platforms and on buses and trams - e.g. in Vienna in *Entwerter* (date coding machines) - and are not valid until this has been done. Ride-at-will tickets are issued by many city transport authorities and the offers included in this book represent only a selection; a popular type of cheap city travel is offered by the purchase of books of tickets which in effect give one or two free rides.

City Transport Zones

A number of cities issue ride-at-will tickets which are valid for a series of zones emanating from the centre and extending into the suburbs. Tickets may be purchased for a central zone, any one zone or a combination of zones.

Dates

Where the holder is required to validate a European transport pass by inscribing the date of travel, this must always be done in the order Day-Month-Year and not in the form Month-Day-Year used in North America.

Exchange Orders

Travel agents sometimes obtain passes by issuing an exchange order or voucher on an office of the transport company offering the reduced-rate travel and may therefore require several days' notice. Some passes are issued only in the country concerned and offices abroad must issue a voucher which is exchanged for the pass on arrival. Intending purchasers of rail passes may have to break their journey at a frontier station and continue by a later train (refer to "Issues").

5

Exchange Rates

The price of each pass is usually fixed in the national currency and variations in exchange rates may affect the prices charged in other currencies. Exceptions are the Eurailpass and other Eurail reduced-rate tickets, the prices of which are fixed in US dollars; the Inter-Rail Card and Nordturist Ticket, their prices being shown in sterling or local Scandinavian currency but which are calculated in UIC francs (a railway accounting unit); the Hungarian Tourist Ticket and the Greek Tourist Card which have been converted from the ECU (European Currency Unit) rate and reflect the conversion from the ECU to the standard currency shown at the time of going to press. Changes in exchange rates can result in different prices (in comparison) being charged in various countries for the same ticket.

Expiry

Rail passes expire at midnight on their last day of validity unless a different time is shown on the ticket, even if the holder is travelling by an overnight train not scheduled to reach its destination until next morning. On suburban lines the pass will normally be accepted until the end of the day's services, even if after midnight. 24-hour tickets issued or validated by machine will expire 24 hours from the time stamped on them.

Fringe Benefits

In addition to the travel benefits listed in this book, some passes entitle the holder to discounts at certain hotels, restaurants, shops, museums, zoos and other attractions and to reduced-rate sightseeing tours, car rental facilities etc. Details are frequently shown in a leaflet supplied with the ticket or on the ticket cover.

Groups

Most transport companies offer reduced-rate travel for groups travelling together on specific journeys and these tickets may be cheaper than issuing each group member with a travelpass.

Identity Documents

Most passes are personal to the holder who must therefore be able to furnish proof of identity when travelling. In some cases an identity check may require a specimen signature. Always carry your passport or other identity document when using a ticket which bears your name.

Issues

Rail passes take time to issue and cannot be obtained on board a train or a few minutes before a train leaves; some countries specify a minimum of 15 or 30 minutes before train departure times and the more complicated types of ticket may have to be issued at least one day in advance of travel. At some stations, rail passes are issued only at the information counter which may close in the early evening.

Maps

A map showing the area of validity is commonly supplied with a regional pass but not necessarily with a national or international pass. Maps of the railway systems of each country appear in the monthly Thomas Cook

European Timetable or - for travel outside Europe - in the Thomas Cook Overseas Timetable which is published six times a year. The Thomas Cook Rail Map of Europe, published every two years, shows the railways of all countries in Europe, with the Thomas Cook Rail Map of Britain & Ireland covering those two countries in greater detail. The newest addition to this excellent range of maps is the Thomas Cook World Rail Map, depicting lines in every country which operates passenger rail systems. Thomas Cook Publishing also stock a number of country rail maps which are advertised in this publication after or in the text of the country which they cover.

Misuse

The passes listed in this guide are mostly personal and non-transferable. They carry the name of the holder who must be able to provide proof of identity when requested. Passes are liable to be forfeited if presented by anyone other than the person for whom they were issued or if they bear any evidence of alteration or tampering.

Other (Unlisted) Countries

The omission of a country from this guide implies that there are no known air passes or ride-at-will rail tickets available on the national airlines or railway systems of that country. There may however be such tickets on city transport systems which we have not had space to include or deemed to be of sufficient interest.

Private Railways

Rail passes issued for a national rail-way system are not valid on private, local or mountain railways unless a note to the contrary appears on the ticket and in the section concerned.

Proof of Age

May be required for the issue of passes to young persons and senior citizens. A passport or national railcard showing date of birth is usually accepted as proof of age but students may also need a student identity card. Reduced-rate tickets are often available to visiting travellers over the age of 60 or 65 in many countries.

Proof of Residence

Certain tickets require proof of residence either within or outside the country concerned. Examples of proof of residence include a business address card, driving licence, a self-addressed envelope bearing a recent postmark or even a residential telephone or power supply bill.

Railcards

This guide is not intended to cover railcards available to certain categories of rail user (for example students, groups, senior citizens) which allow the holder to purchase rail tickets at reduced rates for travel in his or her *own* country. However a brief mention is included of certain cards which may be of interest to touring visitors.

Refunds

A refund will generally be made only where a pass is surrendered before its commencement of validity and only in the country where it was purchased.

It may however be possible to obtain a partial refund (or extension of validity) in the event of an industrial strike or other suspension of service but the claim must be supported by a certificate bearing the official stamp of the transport authority concerned in the area affected.

Reservations
Possession of a pass does not exempt the holder from obtaining a seat reservation where this is mandatory. Advance reservations are strongly recommended.

Scratch & Ride Tickets
Scratch & Ride tickets are becoming increasingly used on city transport systems for one day or several days' travel on their services. The special covering on the calendar printed on the ticket is scratched off by the user to reveal the year, month and day on which they wish to use it and the ticket then becomes valid for that day.

Season Tickets
This guide is not intended to cover residential season tickets but visitors making an extended stay in an overseas country should enquire locally for details of any available facilities. It is useful to carry spare passport-type photographs for this purpose.

Special Trains
Rail passes cannot be used on non-timetabled trains such as excursions, charter trains or private-sponsored rail tours. However certain passes allow the holder to purchase local excursion tickets at reduced rates.

Standard Class
Is the designation now used in the United Kingdom for the former second class.

Supplements
Holders of all rail passes are required to pay the normal fast train supplements - e.g. EuroCity international trains in Continental Europe - unless a note to the contrary appears in the guidebook section concerned (and on the ticket). The normal supplements must be paid for sleeping car or couchette accommodation. Passes do not include the cost of meals or refreshments.

Symbols - *refer to Editorial, page 3*

Time Restrictions
Area and city day tickets often have restrictions on their use in peak travelling hours and in these cases cannot be used before 0830 or 0930 Mondays to Fridays.

Timings
Timings for scheduled air services can be found in each airline's published timetable. Timings for most mainline rail services in Europe are contained in the Thomas Cook European Timetable and for places outside Europe in the Thomas Cook Overseas Timetable.

Water Transport
As well as passes which are available both on rail and on sea and lake ferry services there are some which are specific to the waterborne services of sea, lake and river transport operators.

EUROPE

InterRail Card

Availability: Available to persons under 26 years of age on the first day of the card's validity who can prove that for the previous six months they have been resident in one of the following countries: Austria, Belgium, Bulgaria, Czechoslovakia, Denmark, Finland, France, Germany, Greece, Hungary, Ireland (Republic), Italy, Luxembourg, Morocco, Netherlands, Norway, Poland, Portugal, Romania, Spain, Sweden, Switzerland, Turkey, the United Kingdom and Yugoslavia together with Algeria, Tunisia and any European country not participating in the InterRail scheme.

Coverage: Gives one month's unlimited 2nd class travel on the national railways of the first 25 countries listed above but excluding the country where the card is purchased. Up to 50% discounts on rail travel and shipping services in the country where the card is purchased . Reductions on a number of cross-Channel, North Sea and Irish Sea ferries and hovercraft, on certain Scandinavian Seaways services to and from Scandinavia, on Irish Ferries services (Ireland-France) and most shipping services Spain-Morocco, mainland France-Corsica and mainland Italy-Sardinia, Hellenic Mediterranean/ Adriatica shipping services between Brindisi and Patras; also certain Swiss mountain railways and other private railways in Switzerland, Germany and Austria

Reduced entry fees to a number of transport museums.

Restrictions/Conditions of Use: Supplements are payable on some express trains.

Cost: £175

Purchase: May be bought from principal railway stations, railway travel centres and appointed agents in the participating countries, including - in the UK - from Thomas Cook. A valid passport must be produced at the time of purchase. To extend validity by more than one month, extra passes may be purchased.

InterRail + 26 Passes 🚋 ⛴

Availability: Available to persons *over* the age of 26. Otherwise coverage and conditions the same as for the ordinary InterRail Card.

Restrictions/Conditions of Use: The 15-day pass does not include travel in Spain, Portugal and Morocco.

Cost: £175 for a 15-day pass; £235 for a one-month pass.

Note: The InterRail + Boat and InterRail Flexi Cards are no longer available.

Rail Europ Senior (RES) Card 🚋 ⛴ 🚌

Availability: A Senior Citizen Railcard which is available to persons aged 60 or over who hold a national senior citizen's railcard issued in one of the following countries: Austria*, Belgium, Denmark*, Finland, France, Germany*, Greece, Hungary*, Ireland (Republic), Italy*, Luxembourg, Netherlands, Norway*, Portugal, Spain, Sweden*, Switzerland, UK (including Northern Ireland) and Yugoslavia*.

Coverage: Gives reduced-rate 1st or 2nd class travel for one year from the date of issue on the rail systems of the above participating countries (including a number of private railways and bus services in Switzerland) and on a number of sea and lake crossings. Allows up to 50% reductions in most participating countries except those marked * above which allow up to 30% reductions.

Restrictions/Conditions of Use: RES cards issued *in* France are not valid for travel between 1500 hours on Friday to 1200 on Saturday and from 1500 hours on Sunday to 1200 on Monday. For RES cards purchased *in* Germany no reductions are allowed for journeys of less than 50 kilometres over the lines of Deutsche Bundesbahn or when tickets are bought from automatic dispensing machines. When RES cards are purchased in Switzerland, reductions on Swiss routes are given for return journeys only. Holders of RES cards must be able to produce their national senior citizen's railcard and passport as well as the RES card on any journey. Validity of the card cannot exceed that of the holder's national senior citizen's card.
Cost: £7.50

Purchase: May be obtained from offices of the national railways of participating countries and their appointed agents.

Eurailpass 🚋 ⛴ 🚌

Availability: Available to persons who can prove that for the previous six months they have been resident outside Europe (but excluding those resident in Algeria, Morocco and Tunisia).

Coverage: Gives unlimited 1st class travel (free of any fast train supplements) for 15 or 21 days or 1-3 months on the national railways of Austria, Belgium, Denmark, Finland, France, Germany, Greece, Hungary, Ireland (Republic), Italy, Luxembourg, Netherlands, Norway, Portugal, Spain, Sweden and Switzerland. Also allows free or reduced-rate travel on certain private railways and certain bus, ferry, river and lake shipping services - including the Rhine and Danube - and ferry crossings between Italy and Greece,

Restrictions/Conditions of Use: Does not cover high season surcharges on Italy-Greece ferries. Before commencing the first journey the holder must present the Eurailpass at a railway station for validation; the railway authorities will enter the dates of validity and the holder's passport number. Presentation of the holder's passport with the Eurailpass is compulsory. The various types of Eurail passes are not valid on certain Swiss narrow gauge and mountain railways; a map showing Eurail routes in Switzerland is supplied with the pass. Passes are not valid on British Rail services.

Cost: 15 days US$390, 21 days US$498, 1 month US$616, 2 months US$840, 3 months US$1042; children aged 4 to 11 half price.

Purchase: May be bought at non-European offices of Rail Europe Inc./French Rail Inc. and German Federal Railways, from CIT Tours in the USA and Canada and their appointed agents outside Europe and from RENFE/Spanish National Railways in South American countries. In the USA Eurail passes may be purchased by post from Forsyth Travel Library whose address and telecommunication details appear on page 96. The Eurailpass is issued with a duplicate or counterfoil card to be filled out at time of validation; this is the proof of purchase and can be used to obtain a replacement pass in the event of loss. the intended first date of validity of the pass.

Eurail Aid Offices

The Eurailpass is not normally sold in Europe but certain principal offices of the participating railways, as well as one office in London (French Railways), act as Eurail Aid offices. In addition to helping Eurailpass holders in difficulty, they can issue the Eurailpass to nationals of non-European countries in which there is no national agent; intending purchasers must produce a passport which clearly shows that they are resident outside Europe and which bears a date stamp (date of departure from an overseas country or date of entry into Europe) not more than six months prior to the intended first date of validity of the pass. They can also deal with Eurailpass holders who wish to extend their stay in Europe against payment of an extra fee (all payments in local currency). This information also extends to the Eurail Saverpass, Flexipass and Youthpass.

Eurail Aid Offices are at the following stations and offices:

AUSTRIA - Wien Westbahnhof, Innsbruck Hauptbahnhof and Salzburg Hbf.

BELGIUM - Brussels Midi Station (Salon d'Accueil Service International).

DENMARK - DSB Travel Agency at Copenhagen Central Station.

FINLAND - Helsinki main station.

FRANCE - Paris Nord & St. Lazare stations, Marseille St. Charles Stn. ("Billets Internationaux" window), Nice-Ville Stn. and SNCF offices at Orly and Roissy-Charles de Gaulle airports.

GERMANY - Berlin Zoologischer Garten Stn., Cologne Hbf., Dresden Hbf., Frankfurt am Main Hbf., Hamburg Hbf., Heidelberg Hbf., Leipzig Hbf., Munich Hbf., Stuttgart Hbf.

GREECE - Hellenic Railways travel office No. 2 at 1 Rue Karolou in Athens; Thessaloniki Stn.

HUNGARY - MAV sales office at 35 Nep Kòz Earsasag Utja in Budapest.

IRELAND - CIE International Rail Ticket Sales Office, 35 Lower Abbey Street, Dublin.
ITALY - The railway stations of Bari Centrale, Florence SMN, Milan Centrale, Naples Centrale, Palermo Centrale, Rome Termini, Venice Santa Lucia.
LUXEMBOURG - Gare de Luxembourg.
NETHERLANDS - Utrecht Central Station information desk.
NORWAY - Oslo Sentral Station.
PORTUGAL - Lisbon Santa Apolonia Stn., Faro Stn., Porto - S. Bento Stn.
SPAIN - RENFE offices at 44 Alcala in Madrid and at Madrid-Barajas International Airport, Barcelona Sants Stn., RENFE offices at 29 Calle Zaragoza in Seville and at 2 Plaza Alfonso el Magnánimo in Valencia.
SWEDEN - Stockholm Central Station.
SWITZERLAND - At the main stations of Basel SBB, Bern, Geneva & Geneva Airport, Lucerne, Zürich & Zürich Airport.
UNITED KINGDOM - French National Railways at 179 Piccadilly, London.

AVAILABLE FROM THOMAS COOK

The Thomas Cook European Timetable is recommended by the Eurailpass authorities in their brochure and available from Thomas Cook in England or from the Forsyth Travel Library in the USA (refer to footnote at the bottom of page 96). Another invaluable aid to the Eurail traveller is the **Thomas Cook Rail Map of Europe;** full details of both these publications appear on page 94.

For details of obtaining the Thomas Cook Publishing sales leaflet and ordering the publications featured on this page refer to footnote on page two.

Eurail Saverpass

Availability: Same as for the Eurailpass but issued to groups of three or more persons travelling together throughout their tour; also available to two people travelling together but only between October 1 and March 31.

Coverage: As for the Eurailpass; valid for 15 consecutive days of 1st class travel.

Restrictions/Conditions of Use: One person must hold a Master Ticket or Control Voucher cross-referenced to the individual travel tickets.

Cost: US$298 per person.

Purchase: As for the Eurailpass.

Eurail Flexipass

Coverage: As for the Eurailpass; valid for 1st class travel on any 5 days within a specified 15-day period, any 9 days within 21 or any 14 days within one month.

Cost: 5 days US$230, 9 days US$398, 14 days US$498; children aged 4-11 at half price.

All other details as per the Eurailpass.

Eurail Youthpass & Youth Flexipass

Availability: Available to persons under 26 years of age who can prove that for the previous six months they have been resident outside Europe (but excluding Algeria, Morocco and Tunisia).

Coverage: Gives unlimited 2nd class travel - free of any fast train supplements - on the same transport systems as for Eurailpass. The Youthpass is valid for one or two months and the Youth Flexipass for any 15 days or any 30 days in a 3-month period.

Cost: Youthpass - 1 month US$425, 2 months US$540; Youth Flexipass - 15 days in 3 months US$340, 30 days in 3-months US$540

All other details as per the Eurailpass.

Note covering all Eurail passes:
Whilst free reservations can be made at railway stations and offices this does not necessarily apply to authorised agents.

Eurail Bonuses
Austria: Free travel on Schneeberg and Schafberg rack railways and on Wolfgangsee ships and DDSG Danube steamers between Passau & Vienna. 50% reduction on Lake Constance (Bodensee) steamers.

Denmark: Free travel on DB, DSB and SJ train and car ferries and on Stena Line ships between Frederikshavn and Göteborg. 50% reduction on Copenhagen-Malmö Flyvebådene hydrofoils (25% for Youthpass holders); 30% reduction on KDS Hirtshals-Kristiansand ferry; 20% reduction on DFDS/Scandinavian Seaways services to and from England and the Faeroe Isles as well as between Copenhagen and Oslo. For reductions on other ferry crossings refer to section for Germany.

Finland: Free travel on Silja Line Helsinki-Stockholm and Turku-Åland Islands-Stockholm services (normal charges apply for cabins and berths).

France: Free travel on Irish Ferries services to and from Ireland but normal port taxes and cabin & reserved seat charges apply; advance reservation is necessary for the months of July and August and at all times when cabin accommodation is requested. Free travel on the Chemins de Fer de la Provence line Digne-Nice.

Germany: Free travel on Puttgarden-Rødby, Warnemünde-Gedser and Sassnitz-Trelleborg ferries; on regular daily trips of KD German Rhine Line steamers between Cologne & Mainz and Koblenz & Cochem (extra charge for hydrofoil services); Europabus lines 189 (Castle Road) Mannheim-Nuremberg and 190 (Romantic Road) Frankfurt/Main-Füssen/Munich. 50% reduction on TT Line Travemünde-Trelleborg ferries, on Lake Constance (Bodensee) steamers and on the Schauinsland mountain railway. 40% reduction for Youthpass holders on the roundtrip bus fare for the journey Braunschweig-Berlin operated by Bayern Express/Kuhn Berlin GmbH.

Greece: Free travel on ships of Hellenic Mediterranean and Adriatica Lines between Patras and Brindisi except during the period June 10-September 30 when a high season surcharge is payable; during July and August advanced reservation is recommended and the reservation fee, reserved seats & cabins and port taxes are extra. 30% reduction on Adriatica Line services between Piraeus-Candia-Venice or Alexandria (not valid on the Piraeus-Candia section).

Ireland: Free travel on Irish Ferries services - refer to the section for France. Free travel on Expressway bus services owned and operated by CIE except those operated jointly to and from Northern Ireland.

Italy: Free travel on Hellenic Mediterranean/Adriatica crossing between Italy and Greece as detailed under the section for Greece. 30% reduction on Adriatica Line sailings Venice-Piraeus-Candia-Alexandria as given under Greece. 10% reduction on CIT guided sightseeing tours in a number of cities.

Norway: 30% reduction on KDS sailings Kristiansand-Hirtshals.

Sweden: Free travel on Silja Line ferries (refer to Finland) and on ferry crossings to and from Denmark and Germany - refer to the sections for those countries. 50% reduction on hydrofoil services to Copenhagen (for Youthpass holders) and the TT Line ferry to Germany - refer to sections for Denmark and Germany.

Switzerland: Free travel on regular steamer services operating on Lakes Biel, Brienz, Geneva, Lucerne, Murten, Neuchâtel, Thun and Zürich, on the Rhine between Schaffhausen and Kreuzlingen and on the Aare between Biel/Bienne and Solothurn. 50% reduction on Lake Constance (Bodensee) steamer services between Romanshorn and Friedrichshafen and between Rorschach and Lindau.

Note: Reductions are only available on ordinary full fares.

Also available in North America is the *EurailDrive Pass* which combines the benefits of the Eurailpass with Hertz car rental.

A list of the countries and cities where Eurail tickets may be purchased can be found on page 95.

European East Pass ▭▭▭

Availability: Available only in North America and sold as a FlexiPass.

Coverage: Offers unlimited 1st class rail travel for 5 or 10 days in Austria, Czechoslovakia, Hungary and Poland.

Restrictions/Conditions of Use: Passes must be validated within 6 months of the date of issue and prior to the first journey and when presented to a railway ticket office must be accompanied by a passport.

Cost: Any 5 days in a 15-day period US$160, any 10 days in a 1-month period US$259

Purchase: Can be bought from offices of

FrenchRail Inc./Rail Europe and their appointed agents in North America. Also by post from Forsyth Travel Library whose address and telecommunication details are on page 96.

Scanrail Pass/Nordturist Ticket and BritFrance RailPass.

Though valid in more than one country and therefore to be classed as international passes, we have included them under Country headings - Denmark, Finland, Norway and Sweden, France and the United Kingdom.

EastRail Pass 🚋

Availability: Available for rail travellers visiting five European countries provided a ret-urn ticket is held to the frontier point of the first country where the EastRail Pass is valid.

Coverage: Valid for 15 days' unlimited 2nd class travel in Czechoslovakia, Denmark, eastern Germany, Hungary and Poland. Also valid on railway-operated ferries in Denmark and to and from Denmark.

Restrictions/Conditions of Use: Does not cover some fast train supplements. 1st class travel is possible on payment of the full difference between 2nd and 1st class fares for the journey undertaken. Passholder must enter the date of travel, starting and terminating points and the route to be taken before each journey. Holders must be able to prove identity to ticket examination staff.

Cost: £120, children aged 4 to 11 half price. Price in Denmark is Dkr1300.

Purchase: From the railway authorities in the countries concerned and from main sales offices and outlets of railway authorities in other European countries. A £4 rebate for adults and £2 for children is allowed when the ticket is returned to the issuing office after use.

NORTH AMERICA

Visit America Fares (Air Canada) ✈

Availability: Available to permanent residents of countries outside North America whose travel - by scheduled service of a commercial air carrier or Air Canada charter flight - originates and terminates outside North America.

Coverage: Valid only for travel within North America on scheduled services of Air Canada and their associated connector airlines in Canada as well as Delta, Cayman Airways and Alaska Airlines.

Restrictions/Conditions of Use: Proof of residence outside North America is essential. Accompanying children must have the same number of flight coupons as adults.

Cost: High season - Adult C$600*/US$500*, children C$500/US$400. Low season - C$500*/US$400*, children C$400/US$325.
* *Based on 2 coupons; additional coupons up to a maximum of 8 may be purchased at C$50/US$40 each.*
High season dates are June 1-Sept. 30; remainder of year is low season.

Purchase: May be bought from Air Canada and their authorised agents outside North America.

Canadian Airlines International also offer "VUSA" (Visit USA) fares with similar conditions to Air Canada's Visit America fares.

SOUTH AMERICA

Amerbuspass 🚌
There are several types of Amerbuspass

tickets offering reduced-rate travel on long-distance motor coaches in the South American Amerbuspass network. Details from T.I.S.A. Internacional/A.L.E.T.A.I.P.*, Casilla Correo Nr. 40, ZIP.1401 - Buenos Aires, Argentina; telephone (1) 276591, 406734, telex 33-17870 or 33-9900.

* *Asociación Latinoamericana de Empresarios de Transporte Automotor Internacional de Pasajeros.*

COUNTRY, REGIONAL & URBAN (CITY) PASSES

ARGENTINA

Argenpass 🚂/🚌

Argentine Railways (Ferrocarriles Argentinos) issue an Argenpass and Youth Argenpass available to visitors to the country.

There is also an Argentine Amer-buspass offering reduced rate travel by motor coach and rail within Argentina.

Details can be obtained from T.I.S.A. Internacional at the address given under "International Passes - South America".

Visit Argentina Pass (Aerolineas Argentinas) ✈

Availability: Valid to holders of international travel tickets to and from Argentina for non-residents of Argentina.

Coverage: Travel within Argentina on all domestic services of Aerolineas Argentinas. Valid for 30 days.

Restrictions/Conditions of Use: Stopovers permitted as per the number of coupons issued; only one stopover at each place. Each flight/sector will utilize one flight coupon. Once flight tickets have been issued, change of routing incurs a penalty of US$25 for re-issue of tickets.

Cost: 4 flight coupons US$359, 6 flight coupons US$409, 8 flight coupons US$459. Children aged 2 to 11 half fare; infants under 2 not occupying a seat - 10% of adult fare.

Purchase: At any office of Aerolineas Argentinas or their appointed agents outside Argentina. Reservations and purchase of final tickets can be made in Argentina.

AUSTRALIA

Austrailpass 🚂

Availability: Available to anyone permanently residing outside Australia.

Coverage: Gives unlimited 1st class travel for a minimum of 14 days and a maximum of 90 days on Railways of Australia state and interstate trains and railway-operated bus (coach) services throughout Australia; also offers a free seat reservation facility.

Restrictions/Conditions of Use: Sleeping accommodation is an additional charge. Use of the pass must begin within twelve months of the date of issue. Passport numbers are endorsed on the tickets by the railway authorities. On 'The Queenslander' premiums covering sleeping berths and meals are charged at A$150 for the Brisbane-Cairns (and vice versa) journey and A$126 for Brisbane-Townsville and v.v.

Cost: 14 days A$690, 21 days A$850, 30 days A$1050, 60 days A$1460, 90 days A$1680; 7-day extensions A$350 each.

No reductions for children, students or senior citizens.

Purchase: Can be bought in the UK from Thomas Cook **(via Compass - details at foot of page one);** in Canada from Goway Travel in Toronto & Vancouver; in Denmark from Benns Rejser Agency on Copenhagen & Holstebro; in Germany from Tourland-Reisen in Frankfurt/Main, in Hong Kong from Westminster Travel; in Japan from Japan Travel Bureau, South Pacific Tours Development and Toyo World Co. Ltd. in Tokyo; in New Zealand from InterCity New Zealand; in Singapore and Kuala Lumpur from Ken-Air Services; in Thailand from DITS Travel, Bangkok and in the USA from Australia Travel Service/Tour Pacific in Burbank, California.

AVAILABLE FROM THOMAS COOK

Australia by Rail
by Colin Taylor
A handy, illustrated guide to how to make the most of your Austrailpass - with routes, services, itineraries and maps.

1440

Railway Systems of Australia
Published in 1980 on a scale of 1:5 000 000 by the Australian Government division of National Mapping, the maps shows 40,000 km of line (six systems) with category and gauge and with six city enlargements.

1490

What every rail traveller in Australia needs to know is contained in the Thomas Cook publications Overseas Timetable and World Rail Map - full details on page 94

For details of obtaining the Thomas Cook Publishing sales leaflet and ordering the publications featured on this page refer to the footnote on page two.

Budget Austrailpass

Availability: To anyone permanently residing outside Australia.

Coverage: Gives 2nd (economy) class travel with the same coverage as the Austrailpass. Allows the booking of economy class sleeping accommodation where available. Economy class sleepers are currently provided on the 'Trans-Australian', the 'Indian Pacific' and on some trains in Queensland.

Restrictions/Conditions of Use: Sleeping accommodation is an additional charge. Use of the pass must begin within twelve months of the date of issue. Passport numbers are endorsed on the tickets by the railway authorities.

Cost: 14 days A$415, 21 days A$535, 30 days A$650, 60 days A$930, 90 days 1070; 7-day extensions A$225. No reductions for children, students or senior citizens.

Purchase: As for the Austrailpass.

Kangaroo 'Road 'n Rail' Pass

Availability: To all overseas visitors to Australia.

Coverage: Allows travel anywhere on mainland Australia on trains and road services of Railways of Australia and motor coach services of Greyhound Australia (including Ayers Rock services) within specified periods of 14, 21 and 28 days. Also offers discounts on some city sightseeing tours.

Restrictions/Conditions of Use: Not valid in Tasmania.

Cost (Adult only): 14 days - 1st class A$825, economy class A$520; 21 days - 1st class A$990, economy class A$715; 28 days - 1st class A$1210, economy class A$910.

Purchase: Available from overseas agents of Railways of Australia (refer to Austrailpass) and Greyhound Australia - for UK agent refer to "Greyhound Australia" section. Can also be obtained in the UK from Thomas Cook **(via Compass - details at foot of page three).** Passport must be produced at time of purchase.

Budget 7 (New South Wales)

Availability: Available for unlimited economy class travel for a 7-day period.

Coverage: All services in New South Wales operated by State Rail, including motor coaches.

Restrictions/Conditions of Use: Not available on services operated by the State Transit Authority or on intersystem journeys which extend outside the state of New South Wales.

Cost (Adult only): A$105

Purchase: From State Rail/Countrylink offices and stations and their appointed agents throughout New South Wales.

Sunshine Rail Pass (Queensland)

Availability: Can be used by anyone for 1st or economy class rail travel.

Coverage: Valid for 14, 21 or 30 days unlimited travel on Queensland Railways, including Brisbane suburban services and the Cairns-Kuranda Scenic Rail Tour.

Restrictions/Conditions of Use: The pass must be presented at the ticket office of the departure station for the initial journey for endorsesment of validity dates. Use of the pass must begin within 6 months of the date of issue.

Cost: 14 days - 1st class A$351, economy class A$242, 21 days - 1st class A$432, economy class A$280, 30 days - 1st class A$528, economy class A$351. Half price for children aged 4 to 15 and for students holding a Railways of Australia Student Identification Card.

Purchase: From main railway stations and sales offices in Queensland.

Victoria Pass

Availability: Available to anyone for 14 days travel within the state of Victoria.

Coverage: Unlimited 1st class travel on Country (V-Line) trains and motor coaches in Victoria; also certain car rental and hotel discounts.
Other V-Line reduced-rate offers include off-peak Super Savers, Family and Youth Savers.

Cost: A$120; half price for children under 16.

Purchase: From the V-Line Travel Office in Collins Street, Melbourne and at Spencer Street & Flinders Street V-Line stations in Melbourne as well as from railway stations in Ballarat, Bendigo, Geelong, Wangaratta and Wodonga.

7-day pass
Available at A$69 to overseas visitors to Australia from V-Line Travel in Melbourne (Spencer St., Flinders St. and Collins St.) on presentation of passport and return air ticket.

Westrailpass
(Western Australia)
Availability: Available to anyone for 14 days, 1 or 3 months travel in the state of Western Australia.

Coverage: Unlimited travel on all road and rail passenger services operated by the Western Australia Government Railways Commission (Westrail).

Cost: 14 days A$215, 1 month A$310, 3 months A$600. (Prices subject to review in July 1991).

Purchase: Can be obtained from Westrail Travel Centres and staffed railway stations.

Bus Australia Pass
Availability: Available to anyone apart from the exceptions listed against 7 and 10 day passes.

Coverage: Valid throughout Australia on Bus Australia and Intertour routes. Provides discounts on certain sightseeing day tours in Adelaide and Perth; 30% discount on Kakadu tours.

Restrictions/Conditions of Use: The 7 and

10 day passes are not available to Australian citizens. The pass is subject to a 10% surcharge if purchased in Australia.

Cost (Adults):
7 days-A$302; 10 days A$384; 15 days - A$486; 21 days A$661; 30 days - A$814; 60 days A$1337; 90 days - A$1802.
10% discount for children under 16, senior citizens and students.
Extensions (minimum of 2 days) are available at A$26 per day.
Purchase: From Bus Australia or Intertour offices or from their agents in main cities in Australia (10% premium if purchased in Australia). Bus Australia have representatives in Asia, Europe, New Zealand and North America. UK agents are Australian Destination Centre, 27 High Street, Windsor SL4 1LH (☎0753-855457; fax 0753-830629); also Rainbow Holidays, Ryedale Building, Piccadilly, York YO1 1PN (☎ 0904-611890; fax 0904-611896).

Bus Australia Flexi Pass
Availability: Available to anyone.

Coverage: Offers flexible travel arrangements within specified sections of Australia as shown under each pass. Journeys may be started at any point and there are an unlimited number of stopovers within the itinerary. 30% discount on Kakadu tours.

Restrictions/Conditions of Use: Backtracking is not permitted except where specified. Apart from the first three, all passes are valid for six months. Travel must commence within six months of date of issue of the pass.

Aussie Discoverer

Valid for 12 months and providing unlimited stopovers at specified destinations throughout Australia.
Cost: A$857

Eastern Discoverer

Valid for 12 months. Australia east of a line Darwin-Alice Springs-Yulara (Ayers Rock)-Adelaide.
Cost: A$545

Eastern Highlights

As for Eastern Discoverer but omitting Darwin.
Cost: A$480

Western Discoverer

Valid for 12 months. Australia west of a line Darwin-Alice Springs-Yulara (Ayers Rock)-Adelaide.
Cost: A$545

North West Frontier

Darwin, Katherine, Broome, Exmouth, Perth.
Cost: A$290

The Outback

Darwin, Katherine, Alice Springs, Yulara (Ayers Rock), Coober Pedy, Adelaide.
Cost: A$278

Northern Discoverer

Cairns, Townsville, Alice Springs, Yulara (Ayers Rock), Coober Pedy, Adelaide.
Cost: A$258 (optional extension to Darwin A$100 return).

Sou'Easter

Adelaide, Melbourne, Sydney, Brisbane, Townsville, Cairns.
Cost: A$257 from Adelaide, A$225 from Melbourne, A$140 from Sydney, A$120 from Brisbane.

Across the Top

Cairns, Townsville, Katherine, Darwin, Broome, Exmouth, Perth.
Cost: A$442

Up Top Down Under

Sydney, Brisbane, Townsville, Cairns, Alice Springs, Yulara (Ayers Rock).
Cost: A$350 from Sydney, A$310 from Brisbane, (Extension to Darwin A$100 return).

Nullarbor Experience

Perth, Adelaide, Melbourne, Sydney.
Cost: A$243

The Centre

Melbourne/Sydney, Adelaide, Coober Pedy, Yulara (Ayers Rock), Alice Springs.
Cost: A$250 from Sydney, A$201 from Melbourne, A$170 from Adelaide.

East Coast Wanderer

Sydney, Gold Coast, Brisbane, Cairns.
Cost: A$140

The Track

Darwin, Katherine, Alice Springs, Yulara (Ayers Rock).
Cost: A$160

Reef & Gulf

Sydney, Brisbane, Townsville, Cairns, Katherine, Darwin.
Cost: A$272

Reef & Rock

Cairns, Townsville, Alice Springs, Yulara (Ayers Rock).
Cost: A$180 (Extension to Darwin A$100 return).

The Alice

Perth, Adelaide, Coober Pedy, Yulara (Ayers Rock).
Cost: A$296

East West

Perth, Adelaide, Yulara (Ayers Rock), Alice Springs, Townsville, Cairns.
Cost: A$470 (Extension to Darwin A$100 return).

Gulf Trek

Cairns, Townsville, Katherine, Darwin.
Cost: A$147

Tasmanian Wilderness

A 14-day pass covering the whole of Tasmania.
Cost: A$139

Purchase: As for the Bus Australia Pass.

Pioneer Aussiepass 🚌

Availability: Available to anyone with the exception of 7 and 10 day passes.

Coverage: Unlimited travel by Pioneer motor coaches and their associated companies' coach services throughout Australia for periods varying from 7 to 120 days. Includes discounts on selected whole and half day sightseeing tours.

Restrictions/Conditions of Use: 7 and 10 days passes cannot be purchased in Australia. The pass must be used within six months of the date of issue.

Cost:	Adult	Child (aged 4 to 14)
7 days	A$302	A$242
10 days	A$384	A$307
15 days	A$486	A$389
21 days	A$661	A$529
30 days	A$814	A$651
60 days	A$1337	A$1070
90 days	A$1802	A$1442
120 days	A$1980	A$1584

Purchase: All passes except those for 7 and 10 days may be purchased from Pioneer and their appointed agents in Australia but at a higher rate than those shown above which are the prices applying to passes sold outside Australia by Pioneer's overseas agents. In the UK, Pioneer's agents are Southern Cross Travel at 2 The Square, Riverhead, Sevenoaks, Kent TN13 2AA (☎ 0732-740421; fax 0732-740472; telex 957283). Southern Cross also sell the Kangaroo 'Road 'n Rail' Pass amd Greyhound Passes.

Pioneer Aussie Adventure Passes 🚌

Availability: Available only to persons who are permanently resident outside Australia.

Coverage: Offer set itineraries covering all or part of Australia and allowing the user to choose a particular circuit and an unlimited number of stopovers. Valid up to 6 months unless stated otherwise.

Restrictions/Conditions of Use: No child rates.

The All Round Adventure

Covers a circuitous route around mainland Australia including major cities, Alice Springs and Ayers Rock.
Cost: A$855; Optional Kakadu National Park & Yellow Waters Cruise at A$80.

The Great Adventure

Covers the eastern part of Australia including Darwin, Alice Springs, Ayers Rock and Adelaide.
Cost: A$565

West Coast Adventure

The western part of the country and as far east as Darwin, Alice Springs, Ayers Rock and Adelaide.
Cost: A$612

East Coast Adventure

Covers Sydney-Melbourne-Adelaide-Coober Pedy-Ayers Rock-Alice Springs-Townsville-Brisbane-Sydney.
Cost: A$545

North West Adventure
North west coast of Australia from Perth to Darwin.
Cost: A$290
North Coast Pass
One-way pass between Coolangatta and Cairns or vice versa; valid for 30 days.
Cost: A$135
East Coast Pass
One-way pass between Sydney-Cairns or Melbourne-Cairns; valid for 30 days.
Cost: A$140 from Sydney; A$225 from Melbourne.
South East Adventure/Pacific Coaster
One-way coverage Adelaide–Cairns or v.v.; valid for 30 days.
Cost: A$225
Top Rock Adventure
Cairns/Townsville-Alice Springs/Yulara (Ayers Rock)
Cost: A$275. Optional extension to Darwin A$100 return and Yulara-Adelaide A$150

Purchase: May be bought only from Pioneer agents outside Australia.

Note: Greyhound Australia and Pioneer have amalgamated into a company known as Australian Coachlines but still operate their own coach networks throughout Australia.

Greyhound Australia

Availability: Greyhound Australia offer Bus Passes and Aussie Explorer Passes which are available to anyone.

Bus Pass

Coverage: Valid for periods of between 7 and 120 days on their own and associated companies' motor coach services throughout Australia.

Restrictions/Conditions of Use and Cost: As for Pioneer Aussiepasses.

Purchase: From Greyhound Australia offices and sales outlets in Australia and from their agents outside Australia. In the UK from Thomas Cook **(via Compass - details at foot of page one),** from Greyhound International Travel in East Grinstead (☎ 0342-317317; fax 0342-28519; telex 8813685) and from South Cross Travel (refer to Pioneer Aussiepass). In the USA from Greyhound International Travel Inc. at 785 Market Street, San Francisco.

Aussie Explorer Passes
Coverage: A selection of set itineraries which between them cover the whole of Australia, many of them similar to Pioneer Aussie Adventure passes. Valid for up to 6 months. 15% discount on certain day tours in Adelaide included in some passes.

Restrictions/Conditions of Use: No child fares.

Ultimate All Aussie Holiday A$855
Best of the West A$612
Best of the East* A$545
Northwest Highlights (Darwin-Perth) A$290
Queensland Explorer A$316
Best of the Outback A$275
Top End Down Under (Cairns-Perth) A$440
Wine, Rock & Reef* (Adelaide-Central Australia-Cairns) A$360.
Southern Highspots (Adelaide-Brisbane) AS120
Sunseeker (Queensland Coast) - from Brisbane A$135, from Sydney A$140, from Melbourne AS225, from Adelaide

AS255.

Heart of Australia (Re-named **Central Explorer)** - from Sydney A$250, from Melbourne A$200, from Adelaide A$170. Extension to Darwin from Alice Springs A$180 return.

Reefender (Darwin-Queensland-Sydney) A$270

North of Capricorn (Darwin-Townsville-Cairns) A$145

Trans Aussie* (Queensland-Central Australia-Adelaide-Perth) A$470.

Aussie Highlights (Eastern half of Australia) A$565

Aussie Rock & Reef* (Central Australia-Queensland) A$410

The Rock Track (Darwin-Alice Springs-Yulara (Ayers Rock)) A$160

Nullarbor Explorer A$240

* Optional extra to Darwin A$100 return.

Note: At the time of going to press a number of passes had been added to the list of Explorer Passes; they include **Go West, Outback and Reef Explorer, Central Coaster, Reef Explorer, Princes Pass, The Monkey Mia Experience, Western Explorer, Coast to Coast, Country Road and Top End Explorer.**

Purchase: As for the Bus Pass.

Down Under Coach Pass 🚌
(Greyhound Australia/Mount Cook Line - New Zealand)

Availability: Available on the above companies' express motor coach networks and on the services of their associated companies in Australia and New Zealand.

Coverage: Unlimited travel for periods of 9 to 45 days. Discounts available on some

sightseeing tours.

Restrictions/Conditions of Use: Passes must be validated at Greyhound and Mount Cook Line offices in Australasia.

Cost:	Adult	Child (aged 4 to 14)
9 days	A$310	A$248
12 days	A$370	A$296
18 days	AS470	A$376
24 days	A$590	A$472
32 days	A$770	A$616
45 days	A$975	A$780

Purchase: Passes (at prices equivalent to the above rates) must be purchased outside Australia - in Canada and the USA, Hong Kong, Japan, Singapore; in the UK the pass may be purchased from Thomas Cook (**via Compass - details at foot of page three**).

Tassie Pass 🚌

Coverage: Offers unlimited travel around Tasmania on all services operated by Tasmanian Redline Coaches, Coastliner and Suncoast Motors.

Cost: 7 days A$99, 14 days A$120, 21 days A$140

Purchase: From offices of the respective coach lines in Tasmania, from Greyhound Australia & Pioneer and from authorised sales agents.

Adelaide - Daytrip Tickets U
Availability: Available to anyone on services of the State Transport Authority of South Australia in Adelaide.

Coverage: Unlimited travel for one day on

the city's metropolitan area network of buses, trains and trams. 10-ride multitrip tickets offering 30% reductions on normal fares are also available.

Restrictions/Conditions of Use: Valid after 0900 Mondays to Fridays; all day Saturdays, Sundays and public holidays.

Cost: Adult A$3.30, child (aged 14 and under) A$1.10

Purchase: Daytrip tickets can be purchased on board buses, trains and trams and from staffed railway stations; multitrip tickets must be purchased in advance and can be bought from the S.T.A. Customer Service Centre, staffed railway stations, S.T.A. bus depots, post offices and selected newsagents and shops.

Transperth Sightseers Ticket *U*

Availability: Available to anyone for travel on the services of Transperth in Perth.

Coverage: Unlimited travel for one or five days on Transperth bus, train and ferry services. Also entitles the holder to reductions in admission prices to a number of tourist attractions as well as certain Swan River cruises. Other reduced-rate offers include Multi-Rider tickets.

Restrictions/Conditions of Use: Cannot be used before 0800

Cost: 1 day ticket A$4.60, 5 days A$19.40

Purchase: From Transperth information offices, staffed railway stations and Western Australia tourist centres.

SydneyPass *U*

Availability: Available to anyone resident outside Australia.

Coverage: Provides 3 days unlimited travel on Sydney's urban transport system operated by State Transit, including city buses, the sightseeing Sydney Explorer Bus, the Airport Express Bus, Inner Harbour and Manly ferries (including Hydrofoil and JetCat) and Sydney Harbour cruises.

Cost: Adults A$35, children (15 years and under) A$20

Purchase: From Sydney International Airport (from Travellers Information Service Office and from the ANSETT Gift Shop in the Domestic Terminal), Country-Link Travel Centres at a number of railway stations and at Circular Quay, Manly Wharf and Circular Quay ferry terminals, on board Sydney Explorer and Airport Express buses, Sydney Coach Terminal, Kings Cross Tourist Information Centre, QANTAS Airways in Market Street and from other locations where the "Sydney-Pass" logo is displayed. Passport or other proof of overseas identity is required.

Metro Passes (Tasmania)

Availability: Various types of reduced-rate travel tickets are available on the services of the Metropolitan Transport Trust Tasmania.

Coverage: Day Rover, Day Tripper and an All Day Visitor ticket offer unlimited travel on Metro buses throughout Tasmania. All Day Visitor tickets afford travel without any time (peak travel) restrictions. Day Rovers can be used within certain time restrictions; Day Rover 10 - ten rovers on one ticket. Day Tripper and Day Tripper 10 tickets with similar coverage as for Rovers are for senior citizens. There are also Metro 10 tickets giving ten trips at discounted prices.

Restrictions/Conditions of Use: Day Rover and Day Tripper tickets can only be used between 0900 and 1630 and after 1800 Mondays to Fridays; any time at weekend and on public holidays.

Cost: Day Visitor 'All Day' A$4.30 Adult and A$2.20 Child (aged 6-15); Day-Rover 'Off-Peak' A$2.20, Day Rover 10 A$17.30; Day Tripper 'Off-Peak' A$1.40, Day Tripper 10 A$10.75.

Purchase: Day Rover 10, Day Tripper 10 and Metro 10 tickets must be purchased from MTT sales agents; all other tickets can be bought from bus drivers. In Hobart tickets may be purchased from MTT enquiry desk at the Tourist Bureau and from a number of shops and newsagencies; in Launceston from newsagencies.

Australia Pass (Qantas)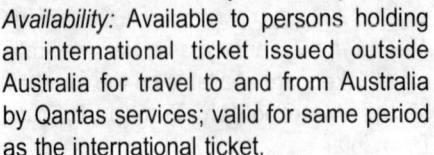

Availability: Available to persons holding an international ticket issued outside Australia for travel to and from Australia by Qantas services; valid for same period as the international ticket.

Coverage: Offers savings of up to 50% on normal domestic fares of Qantas in Economy, Business and First classes.

Restrictions/Conditions of Use: A minimum of three sectors of travel must be purchased; any number of additional sectors may be added. Children between the ages of 2 and 11 pay two-thirds of the full price of the pass.

Cost: For each of the following sectors: Sydney/Melbourne, Sydney/Brisbane, Sydney/Hobart, Melbourne/Hobart, Adelaide/Melbourne, Cairns/Townsville - Economy Class A$110; Business Class A$190; First Class A$250.
For each of the following sectors: Sydney/Adelaide, Melbourne/Brisbane, Brisbane/Cairns - Economy A$160; Business A$260; First A$350.
For each of the following sectors: Sydney/Cairns, Perth/Adelaide, Darwin/Cairns, Darwin/Townsville - Economy A$220, Business A$340, First A$450.
For each of the following sectors: Sydney/Darwin, Sydney/Perth - Economy A$310, Business A$525, First A$700.

Purchase: Passes may be purchased from Qantas and their appointed agents within 30 days of arrival in Australia on proof of overseas residency and valid international return ticket.

Qantas also issue "Discover Australia" fares for overseas visitors on their domestic services in Australia which give savings of up to 50% on normal economy class fares.

South Pacific Pass (Qantas/ Air Pacific) ✈

Availability: For persons holding an international ticket issued outside Australia, Fiji and New Zealand for travel to and from those countries on Qantas or Air Pacific services; valid for same period as the international ticket.

Coverage: Offers savings of up to 50% on normal economy class fares on the services of Qantas in Australia and Qantas & Air Pacific between Australia, Fiji and New Zealand.

Restrictions/Conditions of Use: The passes apply to direct services only. A minimum of three sectors must be purchased, one of which must be an international sector. Any number of additional sectors may be added; sectors may be subject to change without prior notice. Children aged 2 to 11 pay two-thirds of full price of the pass.

Cost: For each of the following sectors: Sydney/Melbourne, Sydney/Brisbane, Sydney/Hobart, Melbourne/Hobart, Adelaide/Melbourne, Cairns/Townsville - A$110.
For each of the following sectors: Sydney/Adelaide, Melbourne/Brisbane, Brisbane/Cairns - A$160.
For each of the following sectors: Sydney/Cairns, Perth/Adelaide, Darwin/ Cairns, Sydney/Auckland, Sydney/ Christchurch, Sydney/Wellington - A$220.
For each of the following sectors: Melbourne/Auckland, Melbourne/Christchurch, Melbourne/Wellington, Brisbane/ Auckland, Brisbane/Christchurch, Brisbane/ Wellington, Auckland/Nadi(Fiji) - A$260.
For each of the following sectors: Perth/Sydney, Hobart/Auckland, Townsville/Auckland, Adelaide/Auckland, Sydney/Nadi, Brisbane/Nadi - A$310.
For each of the following sectors: Cairns/Auckland, Cairns/Christchurch, Melbourne/Nadi - A$360.

Purchase: May be purchased from Qantas, Air Pacific or their appointed agents on arrival in Australia, Fiji or New Zealand upon presentation of proof of overseas residency and valid international return ticket.

Australian Airpass (Australian Airlines) ✈

Availability: Valid for persons arriving in Australia on any international journey who are non-residents of Australia.
Coverage: Based on economy class fares on all domestic services of Australian Airlines.

Restrictions/Conditions of Use: No minimum stay is required but all travel must be completed within 60 days from commencement of first sector.

Cost: Passengers travelling 1 or 2 sectors receive a 25% discount on full fares, 3-4 sectors 30% discount, 5-7 sectors 35% discount and 8 or more sectors 40% discount. A sector or coupon is defined as travel undertaken in one day regardless of the number of flight stages taken. Children aged 2-11 pay 50% of the adult discounted fare.

Purchase: From Australian Airlines offices outside Australia and their appointed agents.

Experience Australia Air Pass (Australian Airlines) ✈

Availability: Only available to non-residents of Australia in conjunction with international fares to and from Australia.

Coverage: Based on a number of set itineraries which offer 40% off the normal economy fares.

Restrictions/Conditions of Use: Travel is permitted in either direction of the itinerary. Minimum stay of 5 days and maximum of 90 days from date of first sector flown. For circular itineraries, travel may commence at any point on the tour. Stopovers only permitted as per fixed itinerary.
Cost: Cairns-Alice Springs-Sydney A$495
Cairns-Alice Springs-Sydney-Cairns A$795
Sydney-Canberra-Melbourne-Coolangatta-Sydney A$550
Sydney-Canberra-Melbourne-Sydney A$330
Sydney-Canberra-Melbourne-Adelaide-Sydney A$520
Perth-Alice Springs-Darwin-Cairns A$735
Perth-Alice Springs-Cairns-Sydney A$795
Sydney-Canberra-Melbourne-Hobart-Sydney A$495
Darwin-Alice Springs-Cairns-Sydney A$730
Darwin-Cairns-Alice Springs-Sydney A$755
Sydney-Melbourne-Coolangatta or Brisbane-Sydney A$500
Sydney-Melbourne-Hobart-Sydney A$455
Sydney-Melbourne-Hobart-Alice Springs-Cairns-Sydney A$935
Sydney-Canberra-Melbourne-Perth A$520
Darwin-Alice Springs-Adelaide-Sydney-Cairns A$910
No child fares.

Purchase: As for Australian Airpass.

Explore Australia Airpass (Ansett Airlines) ✈

Availability: Available to persons perm-

anently resident overseas who are visiting Australia.

Coverage: Economy class on domestic services of Ansett Airlines of Australia, Eastwest Airlines and associated airlines.

Restrictions/Conditions of Use: Maximum stay of 60 days from date of first airpass flight. First flight must be confirmed prior to arrival in Australia. An airpass coupon or flight is defined as travel from origin to destination undertaken on the same day.

Cost: The cost is dependent on the number of flights undertaken so that 3-4 airpass flights or coupons will give a 30% discount on the full economy fare, 5-7 will give a 35% discount and 8 or more a 40% discount.

Purchase: May be purchased from Ansett offices outside Australia and from their authorised agents. A charge is made for re-routing after arrival in Australia.
Ansett also offer a "See Australia" fare which gives international visitors to Australia a 25% discount on their domestic services.

Discover Australia Airpasses (East-West Airlines) ✈

Availability: Available to international visitors irrespective of form of transport to Australia.

Coverage: There are three types of passes - the System Airpass covering all East-West services in eastern Australia, the Northern Airpass covering services north of Sydney and the Southern Airpass in respect of services south of Tamworth/

Sydney. There is also a Trans-Continental Option available on the System & Northern passes and a Red Centre Option on the Northern & Southern passes.

Restrictions/Conditions of Use: Travel to Norfolk Island not allowed on System and Northern Airpasses; travel to Ayers Rock and Alice Springs not allowed on the Northern Airpass. Travel may start or end at any place within the limit of the pass. Only one voluntary stopover allowed in any one place. Maximum usage 21 days.

Cost: System Airpass A$1100; Northern Airpass A$660; Southern Airpass A$460. Trans-Continental Option Perth-Ayers Rock A$235 and Ayers Rock-Cairns A$280. Red Centre Option Sydney-Ayers Rock/Alice Springs-Sydney A$299

Purchase: From East-West/Ansett Airlines and Qantas offices and authorised agents outside Australia.

AUSTRIA

Austria Rail Pass (Bundes-netzkarte)

Availability: Available to anyone not resident in Austria for 1st or 2nd class travel for one month over the Austrian Federal Railways (ÖBB) system.

Coverage: Also covers journeys on the Schneeberg & Schafberg rack railways and ÖBB ships on the Wolfgangsee as well as 50% reductions on Bodensee (Lake Constance) and DDSG (Danube Steamship) services and on a number of private railways. There is also a one-year ticket. Holders of 1st class passes are exempt from paying supplementary charges on EuroCity trains within Austria.

Restrictions/Conditions of Use: Passport or identity document bearing the holder's photograph must be produced when travelling and at time of purchase.

Cost: AS4650 1st class, AS3100 2nd class. No child fares.

Purchase: Obtainable from main station and authorised agents in Austria and from other stations if given advance notice. Appointed agents outside Austria can issue coupons to be exchanged for the Bundesnetzkarte at a main railway station in Austria.

Rabbit Card

Availability: Entitles holder to travel on any 4 days within an overall period of 10 days on Austrian Federal Railways services.

Cost: Adults AS1380 1st class, AS950 2nd class. Youth Cards (for young people aged 6 to 25) 1st class AS860, 2nd class AS590.

Purchase: As for the Rail Pass but is also sold in North America by Rail Europe/French Rail Inc. at White Plains in New York State and by post from Forsyth Travel Library whose address and telecommunication details appear on page 96.

All other details are as for the Bundesnetzkarte.

Kilometerbank Pass

Availability: Can be used by up to 6 persons for 1st or 2nd class travel on Austrian Federal Railways.

Coverage: The kilometric value of the pass is shared by the number of persons travelling with 50% reductions (in kilometres) allowed for children.

Cost: 2nd class - AS1700 for 2000 kilometres of travel, AS2550 for 3000 km, AS3400 for 4000 km and AS4250 for 5000 km. For 1st class travel, 1.5 times the numbers of kilometres travelled is deducted for the total kilometric value of the pass - e.g. a 100 km journey counts as 150 km.

Purchase: From main railway stations in Austria.

Also available is the *Halbpreis-Pass* which costs AS990 and entitles the holder to advertised go-as-you-please "Umwelt-tickets" offering 50% fare reductions.

Regional Rail Pass (Regional-Netzkarte) 🚋

Availability: Available to anyone for unlimited travel for 4 days out of 10 within any one of eighteen different regions of Austrian Federal Railways.; also 50% reductions on a number of private railways. The regions for which passes are issued are:
1 - Arlberg, 2 - Innsbruck, 3 - Kitzbühel, 4 - Drautal, 5 - Gastein, 6 - Salzburg, 7 - Wörthersee, 8 - Salzkammergut, 9 - Innviertel, 10 - Linz, 11 - Murtal, 12 - Alpenvorland, 13 - Waldviertel, 14 Oststeiermark, 15 - Semmering, 16 - Neusiedler See, 17 - Tullnerfeld, 18 - Weinviertel.

Restrictions/Conditions for Use: Passport or identity document bearing the holder's photo must be produced.

Cost: AS500 1st class, AS400 2nd class. 50% reduction for children aged 6-15.

Purchase: From main stations in Austria; also from other stations in advance and from authorised sales agents.

International Rail Passes valid in Austria: All types of Eurail Pass, all types of InterRail Card, Rail Europ Senior Card, European East Pass.

Netzkarte 24 Stunden & 72 Stunden (Vienna) *U*

Availability: Available to anyone for 24 or 72 hours unlimited travel on trams, buses and U-Bahn trains of Wiener Stadtwerke Verkehrsbetriebe in Vienna central zone (Kernzone 100) and in 2nd class travel on ÖBB urban trains in the same area. There is also an 8-day Umweltstreifennetzkarte valid for the same area and consisting of eight one-day travel coupons; several people travelling together on the same day may use these tickets. A Schnupperkarte ticket valid for one day and available for travel between 0800 and 2000 Monday to Friday is being introduced in 1991.

Cost: 24 hours - AS45, 72 hours - AS115. The Umweltstreifennetzkarte costs AS235 and the Schnupperkarte AS35.

Purchase: Tickets may be bought from Wiener Stadtwerke Verkehrsbetriebe information centres at Karlsplatz, Stephansplatz, Philadelphiabrücke and Praterstern U-Bahn stations, from ÖBB Westbahn station (lower level) and ÖBB ticket offices and from sales kiosks displaying *"Tabak/Trafiken"* signs. The Schnupperkarte is not available from ÖBB.

Salzburg Ticket *U*

Coverage: Offers unlimited travel on the city's municipal buses, the fortress funicular, the Mönchsberg-lift and the Salzburg-Bergheim tramway (Lokalbahn) for one or three days.

Restrictions/Conditions of Use: Tickets are valid within the city limits (S-Zone) and out to Bergheim by tram. Ticket must be signed and identification carried by the holder.

Cost: 1 day - AS48, 3 days - AS96; half price for children.

Purchase: From tobacconists, from Salzburger Stadtwerke ticket offices and from the tourist information office.

Touristen-Gesamtnetzkarte (Graz) *U*

Coverage: Gives unlimited travel on trams, buses and the Schlossbergbahn of Grazer Verkehrsbetriebe. Valid for 24 hours from time of validation of the first journey.

Cost: AS42

Purchase: Tickets may be purchased in trams and buses and from a number of sales kiosks.

BELGIUM

Benelux Tourrail Card 🚃

Availability: Available to anyone for unlimited 1st or 2nd class travel over the lines of Belgian National Railways (SNCB). Also valid in Luxembourg and the Netherlands.

Coverage: Allows 5 days of travel within a specified 17-day period. The young person's ticket is marketed as Benelux Tourrail Junior.

Restrictions/Conditions of Use: The ticket must be dated by the holder before commencing travel each day. Passport and specimen signature required; proof of age for all persons under 26.

Cost: Adult (26 +) 1st class - Bfr4180, 2nd class - Bfr2770. Young persons (under 26 years of age) 1st class - Bfr2990, 2nd class Bfr1990. For cost in sterling refer to the section for the Netherlands.

Purchase: From railway stations in Belgium and the other Benelux countries, from Netherlands Railways' offices outside the Netherlands and from appointed sales agents.

Also available is a *Benelux-Weekend Return Ticket,* which allows reductions of 25% for 1 person and 50% for 2-6 persons on ordinary return fares between the three Benelux countries after 1600 hours on a Thursday and up to 2400 hours on a Monday.

Belgian Tourrail Card 🚃

Availability: Valid in 1st or 2nd class on services of Belgian National Railways.
Coverage: 5 days travel within an overall validity of 17 days.

Restrictions/Conditions of Use: The ticket must be dated by the holder before commencing each day's travel. Passport and specimen signature required.

Cost: Adult (26 +) 1st class - Bfr2550, 2nd class - Bfr1700; young persons (under 26)

1st class - Bfr1950, 2nd class - Bfr1300.

Purchase: From railway stations in Belgium and appointed sales agents outside Belgium.

Belgian Half Fare Card 🚃
Also known as a Fixed Rate Reduced Card.
Availability: Available on all scheduled services of Belgian National Railways in 1st or 2nd class.

Coverage: Entitles the holder to a reduction of 50% on the standard rail fare for a period of one month.

Cost: Bfr550. No reductions on childrens' fares.

Purchase: From same outlets and with same requirements as the Belgian Tourrail Card.

Belgian 16-Day Runabout Ticket 🚃
Also known as a Season Ticket.
Coverage: Gives 16 consecutive days unlimited 1st or 2nd class travel on Belgian National Railways.

Cost: 1st class - Bfr4920, 2nd class - Bfr3280. No reductions for children.

All other details as for the previous three cards.

International Rail Passes valid in Belgium: All types of Eurail Pass and InterRail Cards, Europ Senior Card (plus Benelux travel cards and tickets).

Carte TTB 🚃 🚌
Availability: Valid for unlimited travel on train, tram and bus services of Belgian National Railways (NMBS/SNCB), Vlaamse Vervoer Maatschappij (VVM - De Lijn) and Société Regional Wallonne des Transports (SRWT).

Coverage: Any 5 days out of a period of 17 consecutive days.

Cost: Adult (26 +) 1st class - Bfr3050, 2nd class - Bfr2200; young persons (aged 6-25) 1st class - Bfr2350, 2nd class - Bfr 1700

Purchase: From SNCB stations and other public transport authorities in Antwerp, Ghent, Brussels, Charleroi, Liège and Verviers.

24-Hour Card *U*
Availability: Valid for one day's unrestricted travel on the urban services of VVM - De Lijn and SRWT in 25 major towns of Belgium.

Cost: Bfr160 per person

33

Purchase: From offices and appointed sales outlets of the relevant transport companies.

VVM - De Lijn Cards 🚌

Availability: De Lijn (formerly NMVB/SNCV) issue a variety of reduced-rate cards for their bus and tram services operating along the Belgian coast.

Coverage: Individual and Family one-day and 5-day cards are among those on offer. The 5-day cards offer travel on any five days out of 14. The Family card covers any number of children.

Cost: Individual 1 day card Bfr280 and Family Card Bfr650; 5 day individual card Bfr800 and Family Card Bfr1900.

Purchase: Purchased from offices and agents of VVM - De Lijn.

BOLIVIA

Visit Bolivia Pass (Lloyd Aereo Boliviano) ✈

Availability: The VIBOLPASS is sold outside Bolivia in connection with international flights of LAB Airlines to and from Bolivia.

Coverage: Covers Lloyd Aereo Boliviano domestic flights for a maximum of 28 days.

Restrictions/Conditions of Use: Only one stopover per destination is allowed but there is no limit on the amount of time spent at one place.

Cost: US$150 for Adults, US$125 for children.

Purchase: From LAB offices and their authorised sales agents outside Bolivia.

BRAZIL

Brazil Air Pass (Varig Brazilian Airlines) ✈

Availability: May be bought only outside Brazil in conjunction with an international ticket.

Coverage: May be used on domestic services of VARIG Brazilian Airlines or Cruzeiro do Sul. The pass consists of 5 coupons or sectors of travel and a maximum of an additional 4 coupons may be purchased. Valid for 21 days from the date of the first sector flown.

Restrictions/Conditions of Use: Not valid on the shuttle service between Rio de Janeiro and São Paulo. The same sector of travel can not be flown in the same direction more than once. Maximum of 4 hours permitted for connecting flights to count as one coupon.

Cost: US$440 for adults and children; US$44 for infants. Additional coupons (up to a maximum of 4) cost US$100 each; US$10 for infants.

Purchase: From VARIG offices and their appointed agents outside Brazil.

CANADA

Canrailpass & Youth Canrailpass 🚋

Availability: Available to persons permanently resident outside Canada; may be purchased in the United States.

Coverage: Allows unlimited coach class travel on VIA Rail trains for a period of 30 days on a national (System) or eastern regional basis. The System Pass covers the entire VIA Rail network; the Eastern Pass is for travel within the Québec-Windsor corridor and destinations east of Montréal.

Restrictions/Conditions of Use: Not valid for travel on railways other than VIA Rail nor on certain days during the Christmas, New Year and Easter holiday periods. Reservations must be made well in advance. Proof of age required for Youth Canrailpass.

Cost: Canrailpass: High Season* - Adults (aged over 25) C$399 for System Pass, C$239 for Eastern Pass. Low Season - C$269 System Pass, C$159 Eastern Pass.
Youth Canrailpass (aged 2-24): High Season* - C$349 for System Pass, C$199 for Eastern Pass. Low Season - C$229 System Pass, C$139 Eastern Pass.
* *High Season for the System Pass is June 1 to Sept. 30 and for the Eastern Pass June 15 to Sept. 9. Dates outside these are considered low season.*

Purchase: In Canada the passes can be purchased at most VIA Rail stations, their offices and appointed agents. Outside Canada from authorised agents which in the UK includes Thomas Cook (**via Compass - details at foot of page three**). A valid passport must be presented at the time of purchase.

Greyhound Canada Pass 🚌

Availability: Available for motor coach travel in Canada for 7, 15 or 30 days to persons permanently residing outside Canada.

Coverage: On the services of Greyhound Lines of Canada who operate nationwide bus lines west of Toronto; also connecting services of Voyageur Inc. between North Bay & Montréal via Ottawa and between Toronto & Montréal via Kingston.

Restrictions/Conditions of Use: Not valid for travel on Greyhound InterCity Express services or for travel east of Montréal into the Maritime provinces.

Cost: High Season* - 7 days £85, 15 days £130; the 30-day pass at £145 is valid all year. Daily extensions cost £8 per day and must be purchased at the same time as the Canada Pass.
Low Season - 7 days £65, 15 days £100.
* *High Season is June 15 - Sept. 15, all other dates are low season.*

Purchase: From Greyhound offices and sales agents outside Canada; in the UK from Thomas Cook (**via Compass - details at foot of page three**).

Toronto *U*

Availability: Toronto Transit Commission offer unlimited travel on TTC vehicles and subway trains operating within Metropolitan Toronto with their Metropass, Day Pass and Convention Transit Pass.

The Metropass costs C$56.50 per calendar month (e.g. June 1-30) and is valid only for the month for which it is issued. It can be purchased between the 24th day of the previous month and the 4th working day of the month of validity (e.g. June 24-July 4 or 5 for a pass valid in July). It can be purchased from subway stations, most TTC ticket agents and branches of the Canadian Imperial Bank of Commerce as well as the TTC Metropass Photo Office in Sherbourne subway station. A photo identification card costing C$2 must be obtained from the Metropass office in Sherbourne Station.

The Day Pass, a scratch-and-ride ticket, costs C$5 and is valid for one person travelling after 0930 Monday to Friday and all day Saturday; on Sunday and on public holidays, the Day Pass is valid for a group of up to six persons which can be one adult and up to five children under the age of 18 or two adults and up to four children or two unaccompanied adults.

The Convention Transit Ticket is available only to convention delegates travelling in groups.

Vancouver *U*

British Columbia Transit operate buses, passenger ferries and rapid transit services within the Vancouver Regional Transit System and offer a number of reduced-rate travel tickets.

A DayPass is valid for one day's unlimited travel after 0930 Monday to Friday and all day Saturday, Sunday and public holidays. Cost: C$3.50 for Adults, concession fare for children (aged 5-13) and senior citizens is C$1.75

Other facilities include books of FareSaver tickets giving a 10% discount on ordinary fares for any day of travel and one-month zoned FareCard passes.

All passes can be purchased in advance from a number of BC Transit sales outlets throughout the city and DayPasses can be bought on the day of travel from ticket machines in SkyTrain stations and SeaBus terminals.

Similar facilities are available on BC Transit services in Victoria.

Explore North America (Air Canada) ✈

Availability: Available to permanent residents of countries outside North America whose flights originate and terminate outside North America. International travel must be on Air Canada flights.

Coverage: Unlimited travel within North America on scheduled services of Air Canada and their associated connector airlines.

Restrictions/Conditions of Use: Proof of residence outside North America is required. Children must have the same number of coupons as accompanying adult(s). Maximum two stop-overs at any one point.

Cost: High season - Adult C$475*/ US$375*, children (aged 2 to 11) C$450/ US$355. Low season - Adult C$425*/ US$340*; children C$350/US$275.
* Based on 2 coupons; additional coupons up to a maximum of 8 may be pur-

chased at C$50/US$40 each.
High season dates are June 1-Sept. 30; remainder of year is low season.

Purchase: May be bought from Air Canada and their authorised agents outside North America

Connectorpass (Air Canada)
✈

Availability: Available for travel by Air Canada or their Connector (associate) airlines within Canada.

Coverage: Travel within the Canadian network of Air Canada, Air BC, Air Ontario, Air Alliance and Air Nova services for three to six stopovers.

Restrictions/Conditions of Use: No more than one stopover permitted per city. Minimum stay one Saturday or Sunday, maximum stay 30 days. Changes in itinerary permitted for a fee of C$50 with 7 day's notice being required prior to departure and one day's notice after travel has commenced.

Cost: 3 stopovers - C$299, 4 stopovers C$349, 5 stopovers C$399, 6 stopovers C$449; children (aged 2-12) flat rate of C$279.

Purchase: From Air Canada and their associate airlines and appointed agents. Advance purchase of 7 days.

North America Unlimited Travel Pass (Canadian Airlines International) ✈
Availability: Journey must start and end outside North America and valid return tickets must be held on transatlantic services operated by any commercial airline.
Coverage: Valid on all Canadian Airlines scheduled services within Canada and continental (mainland) USA.

Restrictions/Conditions of Use: Maximum of 60 days travel is allowed from commencement of first flight within North America. First coupon must be used within 21 days of arrival in North America. Maximum of 2 stops permitted at any one place.

Cost: High season - Adult C$600 for 2 flight coupons, C$700 for 4 coupons, C$800 for 6 coupons, C$900 for 8 coupons with additional coupons at C$50 per coupon (up to a maximum of 8); children C$500 flat fare. Low season - Adult C$500 per 2 coupons, C$600 per 4 coupons, C$700 for 6 coupons, Can$800 for 8 coupons with additional coupons at C$50 each up to a maximum of 8. There are also special Standby fares and fares which extend the coverage to Hawaii.

Purchase: From any office of Canadian Airlines International or their appointed agents outside North America, including - in the UK - Thomas Cook.

Canadian Airlines International also offer "VUSA" (Visit USA) fares with similar conditions to Air Canada's Visit America fares (refer to "North America" section).

Go-Canadian Pass (Canadian Airlines) ✈
Availability: Available to persons permanently resident outside North America who

are travelling on scheduled Canadian Airlines International services to and from North America..

Coverage: All Canadian International flights within Canada and continental USA. Two flight coupons with optional additional coupons up to a maximum of 8. Valid for a minimum of 7 and a maximum of 60 days.

Restrictions/Conditions of Use: Pass holders may be required to prove residency outside North America by means of passport/visa or government-issued tourist card. Does not include services to North West Territories and the Yukon and those operated by Canadian Airlines associate airlines.

Cost: Two Flight Coupons High Season* - Adult C$475, child C$450; Low Season - Adult C$425, child C$350. Additional adult coupons at C$50 per coupon.
* High season dates are June 1 - Sept. 30; all other dates are low season.

Purchase: From Canadian Airlines International offices and appointed agents outside North America, including - in the UK - Thomas Cook.

CHILE

Visit Chile Passes (LanChile) ✈

Availability: Available to persons residing outside Chile.

Coverage: Each pass covers a fixed itinerary on the domestic services of LanChile starting and finishing at Santiago. Any point in the routing can be omitted and travel can be in either direction. Maximum stay of 21 days (from commencement of first journey).
Continental 1 Pass covers all northern Chile or all southern Chile.
Continental 2 covers the whole of Chile.
Pacific 1 Santiago-Easter Island-Santiago.
Pacific 2 is Northern Chile or southern Chile plus Easter Island.
Pacific 3 - Whole of Chile and Easter Island.

Restrictions/Conditions of Use: Routing changes may be made after the commencement of travel for a charge of US$30 per change. One stopover in each city is allowed with the exception of Santiago where two are permitted for connections.

Cost: Continental 1 - Adult US$250, child US$150; Continental 2 - Adult US$450, child US$270; Pacific 1 - Adult US$812, child US$406; Pacific 2 - Adult US$1000, child US$530; Pacific 3 - Adult US$1200, child US$636.

Purchase: From offices and appointed agents of LanChile outside Chile. Their regional sales office for Europe is in Madrid.

COLOMBIA

Colombia Airpasses (AVIANCA) ✈

Availability: Pass 1 is available only to non-Colombian citizens whose international journey to and from Colombia can be by any carrier; Passes 2 and 3 are available to Colombian citizens who are resident abroad but international travel must be by AVIANCA (Aerovias Nacionales de Colombia S.A.).

Coverage: The three passes cover all domestic services of AVIANCA and SAM (Sociedad Aeronautica de Medellin Consolidada S.A.) within Colombia. Passes 1 and 2 are valid for 30 days; Pass 3 for 8 days but only from January to May and September to November.

Restrictions/Conditions of Use: 10 stops are permitted but no backtracking except in the case of short transit stops. Passes are not refundable.

Cost: Pass 1 - US$325, Pass 2 - US$224, Pass 3 - US$190; children aged 2 to 11 half fares.

Purchase: Must be purchased in conjunction with international travel to and from Colombia from AVIANCA offices and approved agents outside Chile.

CZECHOSLOVAKIA

Prague City Passes *U*

Availability: May be purchased by all visitors to the city.

Coverage: Valid for unlimited travel on trams, buses, the cableway and metro operated by the Prague Transport Company (Dopravni podnik Praha).

Cost: One day pass (valid 24 hours) 25Kcs, two days 40Kcs, three days 50Kcs, four days 60Kcs, five days 70Kcs. Children up to the age of 10 travel free and from 11 to 16 the charge is 1Kc.

Purchase: From city transport sales outlets including a number of newsagents and tobacco kiosks.

International Rail Passes valid in Czechoslovakia: All types of InterRail Cards, EastRail Pass, European East Pass.

DENMARK

Nordturist Ticket 🚋 ⛴

Also known as the Scanrailpass and Nordic Tourist Ticket (Nordturist Med Tag).

Availability: Available to anyone for rail and associated travel in the four Scandinavian countries as long as they are resident outside Scandinavia.

Coverage: Gives unlimited travel in 1st or 2nd class on the national railways of Denmark (DSB), Finland, Norway and Sweden for 21 days. Also valid on railway-owned ferries between Scandinavian ports, on Stena Line services Göteborg-Frederikshavn, Silja Line Stockholm-Turku and Fred Olsen Lines/KDS Kristiansand-Hirtshals, on the bus/ferry route Halden/Sarpsborg-Strömstad and on the NSB bus Trondheim to Storlien. 50% reductions on Silja Line service Stockholm-Helsinki, on Copenhagen-Malmö hydrofoils, on Scan-dinavian Seaways/DFDS Copenhagen-Oslo crossing, on the Larvik Line route Frederikshavn-Larvik, on TT Line sailings Trelleborg-Travemünde, on Vaasa-Umeå ships, on the private railway Hjørring-Hirtshals, on Nord Norway bus services Bodø-Fauske-Narvik-Kirkenes, on Bornholmstrafikken ferries to the island of Bornholm from Copenhagen and Ystad, to Visby on the island of Gotland by Gotland Line, on the Flåm-Bergen route and other services of Fylkesbaatane and on some local buses and boat services in Nordland. Other facilities which the pass offers include free entry to railway museums in Gävle, Hamar, Hyvinge and Odense and discounts of up to 50% at a number of hotels.

Restrictions/Conditions of Use: Does not include seat reservation fees and cabin/berth charges on ferries; also local train services in Stockholm operated by Storstockholms Lokaltrafik (SL).

Cost: Adult (26+) - 1st class £203/Dkr2200, 2nd class £151/Dkr1650; youth (aged 12-25) - 1st class £152/Dkr1650, 2nd class £113/Dkr1250; children (aged 4-11) half the adult rate.

In North America, Scanrailpass charges are Adult - 4 days in 15 1st class US$179, 2nd class US$139; 9 days in 21 1st class US$299, 2nd class US$229; 14 days in one month 1st class US$459, 2nd class US$319.

Purchase: Sold at main railway stations and appointed agents throughout Scandinavia and by the Scandinavian countries' railway and tourist authority offices in other countries. Sold as a Scanrailpass from agents in North America including Forsyth Travel Library whose details are shown on page 96. Passport or other identity document is required at time of purchase and proof of age is necessary for youth tickets.

International Rail Passes valid in Denmark: All types of Eurail Passes and InterRail Cards, Rail Europ Senior Card, Nordturist Ticket and EastRail Pass.

Copenhagen Card *U*
Availability: Available to anyone for unlimited travel on public transport in Copenhagen.

Coverage: Gives unrestricted travel on the buses and suburban trains of Greater Copenhagen for one, two or three days plus free admission to a large number of museums and tourist attractions. Offers 50% discounts on some of the ferry services operating to Sweden (Helsingør-Helsingborg, Dragør-Limhamn, Copenhagen-Landskrona) and 25% discount on the highspeedcraft service Copenhagen-Malmö.

Cost: Adult - 1 day Dkr105, 2 days Dkr170, 3 days Dkr215; children - 1 day Dkr 50, 2 days Dkr85, 3 days Dkr105.

Purchase: From railway stations and city transport offices (HT Kortsalgkontor) in Copenhagen and from appointed agents, shops, kiosks, hotels and tourist offices. Also in Swedish ports which have ferry connections with Copenhagen and the Copenhagen area.

FIJI

Pacific Air Pass (Air Pacific)
✈

Availability: Available only to persons residing in North America. Air Pacific also operate South Pacific One Way add-on fares and a South Pacific Pass in conjunction with Qantas (refer to Australia section for details).

Coverage: For travel within the South Pacific between Apia (Western Samoa), Nuku'alofa (Tonga), Nadi/Suva (Fiji), Honiara (Solomon Islands) and Port Vila (Vanuatu). Offer savings of up to 65% off the normal fares.

Cost: Fiji-Western Samoa/Tonga/Vanuatu US$449. Fiji-Solomon Islands/Western Samoa/Tonga/Vanuatu US$549.

Purchase: From Air Pacific offices and their authorised agents in North America.

FINLAND

Nordturist Ticket 🚃 ⚓
Also known as the Scanrail Pass and Nordic Tourist Ticket
Availability: Available to anyone for rail and associated travel in the four Scandinavian countries provided they are resident outside Scandinavia.

Coverage: Gives unlimited travel in 1st or 2nd class for 21 days on the national railways of the Scandinavian countries and railway-owned ferries between Scandinavian ports; also valid on Silja Line services Turku-Stockholm with 50% reductions on Silja's Helsinki-Stockholm crossings and on Umeå-Vaasa ships. Free entry to Hyvinge railway museum and discounts of up to 50% at a number of hotels. For full details refer to the section for Denmark.

Cost: Adult (26+) - 1st class FiM1434, 2nd class FiM1069; youth (aged 12 to 25) - 1st class FiM1076, 2nd class FiM800; child (aged 4 to 11) - 1st class FiM717, 2nd class FiM536.

All other details: as per the section for Denmark.

Finnrailpass

Availability: Available only to visitors to Finland.

Coverage: Gives unlimited 1st or 2nd class travel for 8, 15 or 22 days on the Finnish State Railways system.

Restrictions/Conditions of Use: Date of validity must be entered on the pass by the issuing authority or by Finnish State Railways (VR) before first journey. Pass holders should have proof of identity when travelling.

Cost: 1st class - 8 days FiM705, 15 days FiM1095, 22 days FiM1380; 2nd class - 8 days FiM470, 15 days FiM730, 22 days FiM920. Children under 17 are entitled to a 50% discount; groups of 3 or more 20% discount.

Purchase: From a number of railway sta-

tions in Finland; outside Finland from offices of Finlandia Travel and other authorised sales agents including - in the USA - Holiday Tours of America in New York and Scantours in Santa Monica, California. Outside Finland coupons are issued and are exchanged for the Finnrailpass in Finland before travelling, at railway stations in Helsinki, Tornio and Vainikkala, at Turku Station or Harbour and at ticket offices in Pietarsaari and Vaasa stations.

International Rail Passes valid in Finland: All types of Eurail passes and InterRail Cards, Rail Europ Senior Card and Nordturist Ticket.

Helsinki *U*

The Helsinki Card is available to anyone and offers unlimited travel for 1 to 3 days in the metropolitan area of Helsinki on buses (including airport services 614 & 615), trams, the metro system and local trains as well as some water buses. Also a free city sightseeing tour, admittance to museums, Helsinki Zoo and other places of tourist interest, reductions at many restaurants, discounts on car hire and free gifts at department stores.

Cost: 1 day - Adults FiM70, children (aged 7-16) FiM40; 2 days - Adults FiM100; 3 days - FiM120. Children half price for 2 and 3 day tickets.

Purchase: The card can be bought at Helsinki Tourist Office in Pohjoisesplanadi, from Helsinki Railway Station (Hotel Booking Centre) and from appointed agents, hotels and Stockmann's department store. In Sweden and Germany it may be purchased from Silja Line in Stockholm,

Hamburg and Lübeck.

The Regional Tourist Ticket gives extended travel coverage on public transport in the city and the region around Helsinki - including Espoo and Vantaa - and on the Suomenlinna ferry.

Cost: A 1-day ticket costs FiM48, 3 days FiM96 and 5 days FiM144 with children aged 7 to 16 at half price.

Sold by Helsinki City Transport offices and the main City Tourist Office.

Holiday Ticket (Finnair)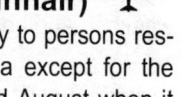

Availability: Available only to persons residing outside Scandinavia except for the months of June, July and August when it can be used by anyone.

Coverage: Unlimited travel on domestic services of Finnair, Karair and Finnaviation (except on Blue Routes) for a maximum period of 15 days. There is also a Youth Holiday Ticket for persons aged 12 to 24.

Cost: US$300; children aged 2-11 half price. Youth Holiday Ticket US$250.

Purchase: From sales offices of Finnair worldwide - including Finland - or from their approved general sales agents.

FRANCE

France Vacances Pass
Marketed in North America as France Railpass or FlexiPass

Availability: Available to anyone permanently residing outside France.

Coverage: Gives unlimited travel in 1st or 2nd class over the rail network of SNCF (French National Railways) for 4 days chosen within a specified period of 15 days or for 9 days within one month. In Paris there are travel concessions on the RATP network including the Metro, buses and RER trains (including free travel on Roissy Rail and Orly Rail services to and from Charles de Gaulle and Orly airports). Reduced rates on "Train + Auto" car hire services, at a number of hotels, historic buildings, museums and tourist attractions, on "Bateaux Parisiens" River Seine cruises and a sightseeing bus tour of Paris. 50% reduction in the fares of the narrow gauge Provence Railways line between Nice and Digne. Also a reduction on Hoverspeed cross-Channel fares if purchased in the UK.

Restrictions/Conditions of Use: The pass includes the cost of all supplementary charges on EC, TGV and TEE express trains within France but not seat reservations or sleeping accommodation charges. The ticket contains one-day coupons or boxes and the holder must enter the date of travel in ink in the "Travel Credit" box each day before using the pass. Each coupon expires at 2400 hours and overnight through journeys starting at any time from 1900 count as one day's travel with the relevant coupon being dated for the following day. The holder must be able to produce proof of identity and residence at time of purchase and during use. The pass is not valid in Corsica.

Cost: 4 days travel out of 15: Adult - 1st class £109/US$179, 2nd class £78/US$119; children (aged 4-11) half price. 9 days travel within one month: Adult - 1st class £195(Child £98)/US$309, 2nd class £134/US$209, child half price.

Purchase: Should be purchased before entering France but is available (on proof of overseas residence) at Paris St. Lazare, Nice and Strasbourg SNCF stations and at SNCF bureaux at Paris-Orly and Paris-Charles de Gaulle airports.

Can be purchased from offices of French Railways and their authorised agents worldwide - in the UK from British Rail Travel Centres, from Hoverspeed at Dover and (in conjunction with an air ticket) from offices of Air France. As well as sales outlets in major cities in North America - including FrenchRail Inc./Rail Europe in White Plains, New York - the pass may be bought by post from the Forsyth Travel Library in Kansas whose address and tele-communication details are shown on page 96.

Other Facilities on French Railways

Carrissimo - gives 50% reduction during the blue period and 20% in the white period of French Railways' Tricoloured Pass Calendar (Calendrier Voyageurs) in 1st or 2nd class for up to 4 young people aged 12 to 25 years travelling together. Not valid on certain TGV trains at peak periods of travel (Reservation band 4). There are two types of ticket, one for 4 journeys and the other for 8; the 4-journey tickey costing Ffr190 and the 8-journey Ffr350.

Carte Kiwi - offers 50% reductions on the regular full adult fare for children under 16 years of age plus one or more (up to a maximum of 4) accompanying adults. The Card is valid in 1st or 2nd class during the white and blue periods of SNCF's Tricol-oured Passenger Calendar and gives un-limited travel on any line of French Rail-

ways system - except Paris suburban trains - and on German Federal Railways network as well as other discount offers. Tickets must be purchased in France from SNCF and the Card costs Ffr360.

The Carte 'Vermeil' offers half price travel to persons over 60 and the *Billet 'Sejour'* 25% reductions on journeys totalling more than 1000 kilometres; issued in France, with the tickets being valid in conjunction with SNCF's Blue, White and Red periods of travel which controls the days of the week that they can be used - e.g. busy weekend and holiday periods.

In North America, Rail Europe/French Rail Inc. market *France Rail'N Drive Pass, France Rail'N Fly Pass and France Fly Rail'N Drive* which offer combinations of rail, car rental and air travel. Also the *BritFrance Railpass* which offers unlim-ited travel on the British and French rail systems plus a cross-Channel journey by hovercraft. A 5-days-out-of-15-days pass costs US$335 1st class, US$249 2nd class, YouthPass (children aged 12 to 25) US$199 2nd class. 10-days-out-of-one-month US$495 1st class, US$375 2nd class and US$299 for 2nd class YouthPass. Children aged 4 to 11 at half the adult fare.

Available from Rail Europe/French Rail Inc. sales outlets in North America inc-luding by post from Forsyth Travel Library whose address and telecommunications details appear on page 96.

International Rail Passes valid in France: All types of Eurail passes and InterRail Cards, Rail Europ Senior Card.

Paris-Visite *U*

Availability: Available to anyone for unlimited 1st class travel on public transport in Paris and the Ile de France area.

Coverage: Gives 3 or 5 days consecutive travel on the SNCF rail network in the Ile de France region, on the RATP/SNCF systems in Paris (Métro, bus and most RER services), on the Montmartre funicular, Metrobus, Noctambus, Orlybus, Orly-Rail, Roissy-Rail airport services, etc. Also various reductions on the prices of some River Seine cruises (Vedettes du Pont Neuf), "Canauxrama", the Grévin Museum, the Tour Montparnasse and Roue Libre bicycle hire.

Restrictions/Conditions of Use: Passes are issued on a zonal basis - maximum of 4 zones.

Cost: 3 zones - Ffr75 for 3 days, Ffr120 for 5 days. 4 zones (including outer zone 4, Versailles and the airport services) - Ffr145 for 3 days and Ffr180 for 5 days.

Purchase: From main Métro and RER stations; from the tourist offices at 53 Quai des Grands Augustins or Place de la Madeleine/Marché aux Fleurs; from SNCF sales outlets at Roissy-Charles de Gaulle & Orly airports, Paris termini and in some major stations outside Paris; from Aéroport de Paris tourist offices at Roissy-Charles de Gaulle and Orly airports.

Formule 1 - Paris *U*

Availability: Available for anyone to travel 2nd class for 1 day on public transport in Paris.

Coverage: One day's unlimited travel on the RATP and SNCF networks in Paris including the Métro, RER services and the Montmartre funicular. Valid for journeys within the four zones of the Paris region, the price depending on the number of zones.

Cost: Zones 1 & 2 - Ffr22; Zones 1, 2 & 3 - Ffr27; all 4 zones (including Versailles) - Ffr39. A 'Formule 1, Zones 1-4 + aéroports' ticket is available at a cost of Ffr66 for travellers who also wish to use the public transport services operating to and from Roissy-Charles de Gaulle and Orly airports.

Purchase: From Métro, SNCF and RER sales outlets in the Paris region.

Carte Orange - Paris *U*

Availability: Available to anyone for unlimited travel for one week or one month on public transport in Paris and its suburbs.

Coverage: Now extended from 5 to 8 zones, the Carte Orange allows unrestricted travel on the Métro, all RER lines, SNCF suburban trains, RATP buses and APTR & ADATRIF services in Paris and the Ile de France region.

Restrictions/Conditions of Use: A passport-type photograph is required.

The monthly ticket is valid for one calendar month - i.e. January 1st to 31st - and is on sale between the 20th and 27th day of the previous month.

Cost: Depends on the class of travel and the number of travel zones required - from 2 to 8. 1991 prices were not available at time of going to press but in 1990 a Zone 1-2 ticket cost Ffr77 in 1st class and Ffr51 2nd class for one week and Ffr270 1st class/Ffr180 2nd class for one month. A 5-zone ticket cost Ffr199 1st class/Ffr112 2nd class for one week and Ffr692 1st class/Ffr391 2nd class for one month.

Purchase: From railway ticket offices, stations and certain bus termini in the Paris region and from authorised agents.

Transport Passes in other French cities
Many cities offer reduced-rate travel to visitors on their urban and suburban public transport networks.
Examples:
Lyon has 40 and 72 hour travel tickets giving unlimited travel on buses, rack railways, funicular and Métro railway systems operated by Société Lyonnaise de Transports en Commun. *Cost:* 48 hours - Ffr45, 72 hours - Ffr63.
Nice - Transports Urbains de Nice sell "Carte Nice Vacances" at Ffr19 for 1 day, Ffr69 for 5 days and Ffr94 for 7 days.
Rouen issues one-monthly bus tickets at Ffr186 (1990 prices).

GERMANY

German Rail Pass

Marketed in North America as the GermanRail FlexiPass
Availability: Available to persons permanently resident outside Germany.

Coverage: Valid for 5, 10 or 15 days' use within a period of one month in 1st or 2nd class on all scheduled Deutsche Bundesbahn and Deutsche Reichsbahn trains including suburban S-Bahn systems which at Düsseldorf and Frankfurt connect the city with the airport. Supplements on fast IC and EC trains within Germany are included. Also covers journeys on most local and provincial bus services operated by DB's regional bus companies and on all long distance domestic motor coach services operated by Deutsche Touring GmbH as well as on day ships of KD German Rhine Line between Cologne and Mainz and between Koblenz and Cochem. There is also a 2nd class Youth Pass for young people aged between 12 and 25.

Restrictions/Conditions of Use: Not valid on private railways, on Motorail trains, on bus services other than those run by DB, on KD hydrofoils or overnight cruise ships. Passport number has to be supplied at time of purchase. The number of days of validity do not have to run consecutively.

Cost: 5 days - 1st class £149, 2nd class £99, Youth Pass (2nd class) £69. 10 days - 1st class £219, 2nd class £149, Youth Pass £89. 15 days - 1st class £259, 2nd class £179, Youth Pass £109. Children aged 4-11 half the adult price.

Purchase: Purchased from authorised agents of German Railways outside Germany including other national railways' sales offices in Europe - in the UK from British Rail's International Travel Centres in London. In North America from Rail Europe/French Rail Inc. in White Plains, New York and by post from Forsyth Travel Library whose address and telecommunication details appear on page 96.

Rail Regional Passes 🚃

Availability: To persons permanently resident outside Germany.

Coverage: Unlimited 2nd class rail travel on all scheduled Deutsche Bundesbahn services for 10 days out of a specified 21 days within a designated region of western Germany for a single person, for 2 persons travelling together or for families. There is a choice of 30 regions and no restrictions on the number of passes purchased.

Restrictions/Conditions of Use: InterCity (IC), EuroCity (EC) and InterCity Express (ICE) supplements are not included in the price. Persons wishing to travel first class must pay the difference between the full 1st and 2nd class fares. The 10 days of travel do not have to run consecutively. Passport number has to be entered on the pass and holder's passport may have to be produced when travelling.

Cost: 1 person - £33; 2 persons travelling together - £44; Family pass* - £55
* Family to consist of one or both parents with any number of unmarried children

under 18 or one or both grandparents travelling with grandchildren.

Purchase: From main DB stations and from German Rail/DER Travel Service sales offices and appointed agents outside Germany.

International Rail Passes valid in Germany: All types of Eurail passes and InterRail Cards, Rail Europ Senior Card and (in eastern Germany) the EastRail Pass.

Samples of Regional Maps - German Rail Regional Pass
1. Heart of the Rhine Valley
2. Munich and Bavarian Alps (West)

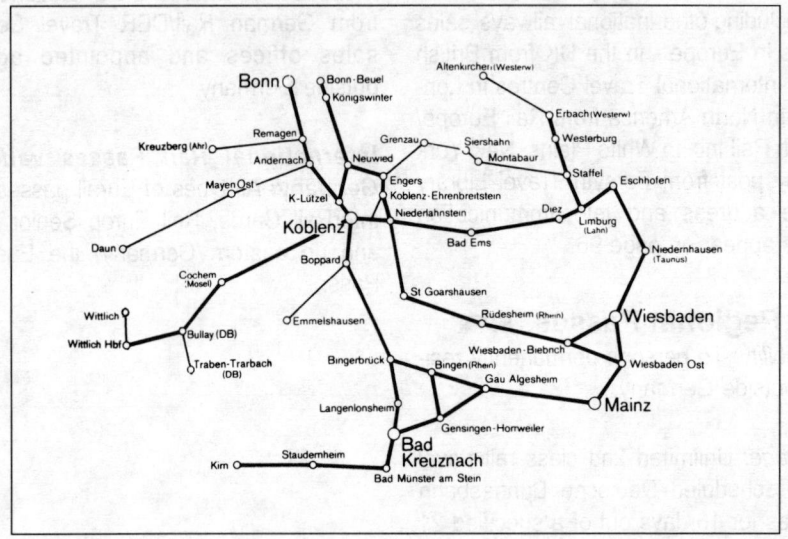

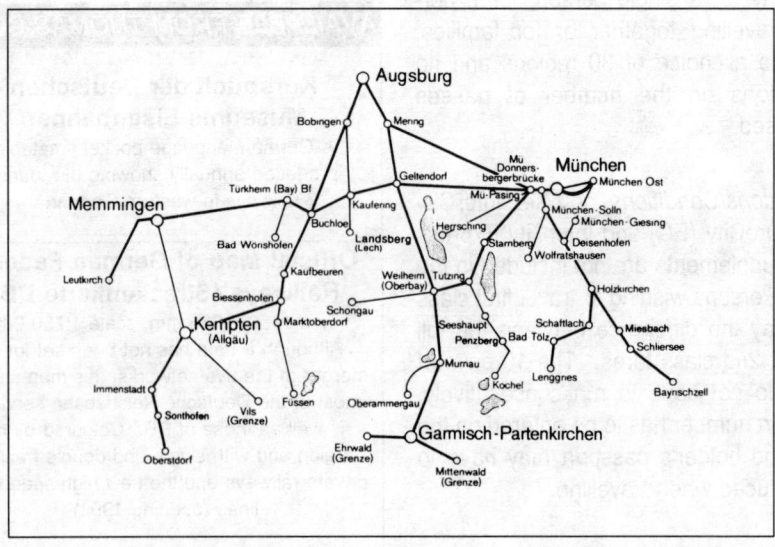

Berlin Touristenfahrkarten *U*

Availability: To anyone travelling on Deutsche Reichsbahn services in Berlin; also bus services operated by BVB and BVG.

Coverage: Tagestariftiket ("Berlin-Ticket") offers reduced-rate travel for one day within the area served by BVG West Berlin transport services and Potsdam City Transport. BVG issue a Family Day Ticket for 2 adults and their children under 16 at weekends and public holidays, a "Ku'damm Ticket" and a Combination Day Ticket (April to October) which is also valid for travel on ferries operated by Stern und Kreisschiffahrt.
Tagestouristenfahrkarte provides similar coverage on BVB East Berlin services, S-Bahn lines and U-Bahn services of urban trains, buses and trams.

Cost: BVG Berlin Ticket - DM9; Family Day Ticket - DM10; Ku'damm Ticket - DM1; Combination Day Ticket - DM16. Tagestouristenfahrkarte for S-Bahn and BVB transport is DM1 and for S-Bahn lines plus the U-Bahn, buses and trams DM2. BVB prices are likely to change after June 30.

Purchase: BVG tickets from ticket counters and vending machines at underground and city railway stations; Ku'damm tickets may also be purchased on board buses. BVB tickets from S-Bahn and U-Bahn stations.

Berchtesgadener Bergbahn
(Jennerbahn/Hirscheckbahn Wanderpass)

Berchtesgadener Bergbahn operate reduced-rate tickets which are available to anyone on their Jennerbahn and Hirscheckbahn mountain railways. The 7-day Wanderpass valid from May to October costs DM49 at the ticket office of the Jennerbahn and offers unlimited travel on both railways. A photograph is required. Family tickets are also available together with a 6-day Wintersports ticket.

Reduced-rate travel tickets in other German cities

Most city and regional public transport undertakings in Germany offer a day ticket suitable for visitors (Tageskarte/24-Stunden Ticket) which is usually valid after 0900 Monday to Friday and all day at weekends and public holidays. Prices vary according to the area covered (often based on travel zones) with some tickets allowing free travel for children of normal fare-paying age. We list below a selection of reduced-rate city transport offers.

Frankfurt. One-day ticket costs DM4 for one zone and 3-day DM12; available from station ticket machines and on buses. There are also "Fahr Bunt" weekly and monthly tickets.

Hamburg. 1991 details not available at time of going to press but in previous years a Day Ticket cost between DM8 and DM12.50 depending on the type of ticket purchased.

Hannover. 24-Hour Ticket costs DM6 in price zone 1, DM10 for entire fare area. One adult holder can be accompanied free of charge by another adult and up to 3 children (aged 4 to 17). Can be purchased from sales outlets throughout the city, automatic ticket machines and on public transport vehicles.

Heidelberg. "Multi-Tickets": DM6 for one day's travel on the city's buses, trams and trains in two inner zones; DM10 for the whole city transport network, this ticket being valid for one person for 36 hours or - at certain times - for 4 persons. Bought from ticket machines and on board vehicles.

Munich. Day tickets are valid for one person but at weekends and public holiday periods may be used by two adults and three children (and even a dog!). DM7.50 for central zone, DM15 for whole transport area; child rates (4-14) DM2.50 and DM4.50.

Stuttgart. Day ticket with no time restrictions covers one adult and a child and costs DM12; a ticket at the same price with weekday time restrictions allows travel by up to four adults. There are also monthly passes for adults and young people.

Rhine-Ruhr. Verkehrsverbund Rhein-Ruhr GmbH offer a Family Dayticket at DM8.50 for travel on public transport services within their operating region.

GREECE

Carte de Tourisme (Greek Tourist Card)

Availability: Available to overseas visitors to Greece for unlimited 2nd class travel on services of Hellenic Railways.

Coverage: Valid for travel on trains of the Greek Railways for periods of 10, 20 or 30 days. Passport or identity card required.

Cost: For 1 person: 10 days Dr9000, 20 days Dr13500, 30 days Dr18000.
2 persons: 10 days Dr15000, 20 days Dr24000, 30 days Dr33000.
3 persons: 10 days Dr19500, 20 days Dr31500, 30 days Dr43500.

4 persons: 10 days Dr22500, 20 days Dr37500, 30 days Dr51000.
5 persons: 10 days Dr25500, 20 days Dr40500, 30 days Dr55500.
No child reductions.

Purchase: May be obtained from main railway stations in Greece and at the international travel offices of the other European railway administrations.

International Rail Passes valid in Greece: All types of Eurail passes and InterRail Cards, Rail Europ Senior Card.

Greek Island Pass

Availability: Available in countries outside Greece for inter-island travel in the Aegean.

Coverage: Valid for a maximum of 5 crossings within a period of 15 days on ships of Hellenic Mediterranean Lines operating between the port of Piraeus and the Aegean Islands, including Paros, Naxos, Ios, Siros, Mykonos, Ikaria, Samos, Thira (Santorini), Astypalea, Amorgos and Tinos, Karpathos, Crete (Heraklion) and Rhodes. Travel is by deck (Third) class which allows for seating accommodation only on board ship (i.e. no sleeping accommodation).

Restrictions/Conditions of Use: Expiry date is two weeks after the date of the first crossing - e.g. first sailing Monday 1st, expiry date Monday 15th. To extend validity, an additional pass is needed. Holder needs to prove identity and residence outside Greece.

Cost: £49 per person.

Purchase: From sales offices of Hellenic Mediterranean Lines outside Greece and their authorised agents.

HONG KONG

Tourist Ticket 🚃

Availability: To all visitors to Hong Kong.

Coverage: Valid on all services of the Mass Transit Railway Corporation (MTR) and the Kowloon-Canton Railway (within Hong Kong).

Restrictions/Conditions of Use: Purchasers must be able to produce valid travel documents, passport or identity card etc. On the last ride, the total value of the ticket can be exceeded regardless of how little value remains.

Cost: HK$25 which is the total fare value of the ticket; each time the holder travels, the fare for that journey is automatically deducted from the value of the ticket.

Purchase: May be bought from Hang Seng minibanks at 8 MTR stations, from all station ticket offices, from MTR travel service centres at 7 MTR stations and from 3 Hong Kong Tourist Association information and gift centres.

HUNGARY

Rail Tourist Ticket (MAV Turista Bérlet) 🚃

Availability: Available to anyone for journeys on the services of Hungarian State Railways (MAV).

Coverage: Gives unlimited 1st or 2nd class travel for 10, 20 or 30 days on the networks of MAV and GySEV Railways.

Cost (in Swiss Francs*): 10 days - 1st class Sfr128, 2nd class Sfr86; 20 days - 1st class Sfr191, 2nd class Sfr128; 30 days - 1st class Sfr256, 2nd class Sfr170.
* or equivalent of country where purchased.

Purchase: Available from main railway stations in Hungary and from the international booking offices of national European railway authorities.

Note: In North America a ***Hungary Flexi-Pass*** is sold by Rail Europe/FrenchRail Inc., costing US$35 for any 5 days in a 15-day period and US$55 for 10 days out of a one-month period.

Lake Balaton Rail Pass (Balaton Bérlet) 🚃

Valid for unlimited 2nd class travel along 131 km of line on the northern shore of Lake Balaton or 104 km of line along the southern shore for a 7 or 10 day period. *Cost:* 7 days Ft640, 10 days Ft960. May be purchased only within Hungary.

International Rail Passes valid in Hungary: All types of Eurail passes and InterRail Cards, Rail Europ Senior Card, EastRail Pass, European East Pass.

Budapest City Passes *U*

Availability: One day passes are available to anyone for unlimited travel on services operated by the Budapest Transport Company (Budapesti Közlekedési Vallalat - BKV).

Restrictions/Conditions of Use: Monthly tickets are issued per calendar month with reductions for tickets purchased after the 15th day of the month.

Cost: One-day: Ft64 for travel on trams, trolley-buses, metro, cogwheel railway and the HEV suburban railway within Budapest ; for same cover plus BKV bus services - Ft80. Monthly tickets cost Ft300 for all types of travel except bus and Ft450 for travel including BKV bus services. There are also one-day and one-month bus only tickets. Prices are expected to rise by an average of 50% during 1991. Reduced rates apply to students and senior citizens.

Purchase: Tickets can be purchased from BKV sales offices and authorised sales outlets through the city.

ICELAND

Bus Passes 🚌

BSÍ (Iceland Bus Central) operate bus services in Iceland and offer two passes on the scheduled network of bus routes in Iceland.

The Omnibus Pass (TIMAMIDI) gives unlimited travel for 1 to 4 weeks throughout Iceland during the summer season from May/June to September. Also available as a 1-week ticket during the off-season period but the routes which can be travelled are necessarily restricted due to weather conditions.
Cost: 1 week summer £120, winter £62; 2 weeks £155; 3 weeks £200, 4 weeks £230.

The Full-circle Passport (HRINGMIDI) is valid for the 'Ring Route' (Road No. 1) around Iceland for the period when this route is open - usually mid May or early June until mid-September - in one direction only (i.e. no backtracking) but with unlimited stopovers and with no time limit on its use. Holders are offered discounts on the cost of a number of coach tours, on camping fees, on horse riding, on ferries and on rates at certain hotels.
Cost: Adult £102; children aged 4-8 at half price and aged 9-11 three-quarters of the adult fare.

Purchase: Both passes may be purchased from the BSÍ Travel bus terminal in Reykjavik (Umferdarmidstödin on Vatnsmyrarvegur) and from BSÍ sales agents. BSÍ also offer air-bus rover tickets for specific journeys within Iceland - refer to following details on air passes.

Air Rover Ticket/Air Passes (Icelandair) ✈

Air Rover Ticket
Availability: Valid for one month on domestic flights in Iceland.

Coverage: Covers routing Reykjavik-Isafjordur-Akureyri-Egilsstadir-Hofn-Reykjavik or vice versa.

Restrictions/Conditions of Use: Travel can commence on any point on the route.

Cost: £137. Children up to 2 years old pay 10% of full fare; 2-12 years 50% (applies to all passes).

Purchase: Sold by Icelandair sales offices worldwide (and their agents) and by Norland Air and East Air within Iceland.

Air Bus Rover
Availability: Valid for specific journeys combining air and bus travel - fly one way, drive the other.

Coverage: Typical itineraries include journeys between Reykjavik and:
Akureyri, Isafjordur, Egilsstadir and Hornafjordur.

Restrictions/Conditions of Use: Valid only between June 1 and Sept. 30. Can be used one way or as a round trip; travel must be completed within 30 days.

Cost of Sample Fares: Reykjavik-Akureyri £69; Reykjavik-Akureyri via Sprengisandur, Akureyri-Reykjavik via Kjalvegur and Reykjavik-Egilsstadir via Akureyri or Hornafjordur £105 each; Reykjavik-Isafjordur £72; Reykjavik-Hornafjordur £80

Purchase: As for the Air Rover Ticket plus BSÍ Travel.

Mini Iceland Air Pass
Availability: A 2-sector pass valid on any segment operated by Icelandair domestic services, Flugfelag Nordurlands, Flugfelag Austurlands and Flugfelag Ernir.

Coverage: Allows unrestricted travel for one month on flights of the above airlines within Iceland.

Restrictions/Conditions of Use: First flight can be booked before holder arrives in Iceland.

Cost: £63

Purchase: Can be bought only outside Iceland by Icelandair international passengers.

Fly As You Please/Iceland Air Pass
Availability/Coverage/Restrictions & Conditions of Use/Purchase: As for the Mini Iceland Air Pass but a 4 sector pass.

Cost: £105

INDIA

Indrail Pass
Availability: Available to any person resident outside India.

Coverage: Gives unlimited travel on Indian Railways for 1, 7, 15, 21, 30, 60 or 90 days in air-conditioned 1st class (AC 1st), Ordinary 1st class and air-conditioned chair car (Ord 1st) and 2nd class (2nd).

Includes fast train supplements and seat & sleeper reservation charges.

Cost:	AC 1st	Ord 1st	2nd
1 day	U$ 65	US$ 29	US$ 12
7 days	US$220	US$110	US$ 55
15 days	US$270	US$135	US$ 65
21 days	US$330	US$165	US$ 75
30 days	US$410	US$205	US$ 90
60 days	US$600	US$300	US$135
90 days	US$800	US$400	US$175

Children aged 5-12 approx. 50% reduction. Rates may vary according to the dollar exchange rate.

Purchase: From the Central Reservation Offices of 16 principal railway stations in India (including Bombay Victoria, New Delhi, Calcutta and Madras) on payment in US dollars or sterling and from Thomas Cook in Bangalore, Bombay, Hyderabad, Madras and New Delhi (one month's notice required, service charge payable). Available in the UK from S.D.E.L. at 21 York House, Empire Way, Wembley, Middx. HA9 0PA; ☎ 081-903 3411, fax 081-903 0392.

Passport or proof of residence outside India must be produced.

INDONESIA

Visit Indonesia Air Pass (Garuda Indonesia Airlines)

Availability: Available to persons permanently residing outside Indonesia who have proof of residence and who hold international tickets to and from Indonesia.

Coverage: For passengers arriving on

Garuda Indonesia or Merpati Nusantara flights at any of Indonesia's gateway cities of Jakarta, Denpasar (Bali), Pontianak, Medan, Biak, Pekanbaru, Padang and Balikpapan and valid on their domestic flights in economy class.

Restrictions/Conditions of Use: Minimum stay 7 days; maximum stay 20 days for VINA 1, 30 days for VINA 2 and 60 days for VINA 3. Only one stopover is permitted at the same place except for transfers or connecting flights within 4 hours. Rerouting is not permitted except to a gateway city on the last domestic flight.

Cost: VINA 1 - US$350 for 4 routes (destinations); VINA 2 - US$500 for 8 routes; VINA 3 - US$600 for 12 routes. Children 60% of the adult fare; infants 10%.

Purchase: From Garuda Indonesia offices outside Indonesia and agents acting on behalf of the airline; also available on arrival at Indonesia's gateway cities provided the passenger has proof of return or continuing international ticket.

IRELAND (Republic)

Emerald Card 🚌 🚌

Availability: Available to anyone for unlimited travel on most public transport services in the Irish Republic.

Coverage: Allows 8 days travel out of a specified period of 15 days or 15 days out of 30 on the services of Irish Rail, Northern Ireland Railways, Bus Eireann (including city services in Cork, Galway, Limerick and Waterford), Dublin Bus - including their Airport and Ferryport services - and Ulsterbus general and Belfast City bus services.

Restrictions/Conditions of Use: Proof of age may be required when purchasing a child card.

Cost: 8 days in 15 - IR£100/Sterling £95*; 15 days in 30 - IR£170/Sterling £161*. Children aged 3 to 15 at half price.
* Subject to fluctuating exchange rate.

Purchase: May be obtained at principal stations and depots of Irish Rail, Northern Ireland Railways, Bus Eireann and Ulsterbus.

For details of the *Irish Rover* refer to the United Kingdom: Northern Ireland section.

Rail Rambler/Road Rambler 🚌/🚌

Availability: Available to anyone for unlimited standard class rail travel on services of Irish Rail and on regular services of Bus Eireann.

Coverage: Both the Rail Rambler and the Road Rambler are valid for 8 days within a specified 15-day period or 15 days out of 30.

Cost: 8 days out of 15 - IR£58; 15 days out of 30 - IR£85. Children 3 to 15 at half price; reduced rates for families.

Purchase: Rail Ramblers can be bought from principal stations and depots of Irish Rail and Road Ramblers from offices of Bus Eireann and authorised agents.

Combined Road & Rail Rambler 🚌 🚌

Availability: Available to anyone for unlimited standard class travel on all scheduled trains of Irish Rail and on regular road services of Bus Eireann.

Coverage: Valid for 8 days travel out of a specified period of 15 days or for 15 days out of 30.

Restrictions/Conditions of Use: Not valid

on Dublin city buses.

Cost: 8 days out of 15 - IR£75; 15 days out of 30 - IR£110. Children aged 3-15 half price; reduced rates for families.

Purchase: From same sales outlets as Rail & Road Ramblers.

International Rail Passes valid in the Irish Republic: All types of Eurail passes, InterRail Cards, Rail Europ Senior Card.

Bus Eireann Rover Ticket

Coverage: Valid on all Bus Eireann scheduled timetable services including city services in Cork, Galway, Limerick and Waterford for any 3 days travel out of an 8-day period.

Restrictions/Conditions of Use: Not valid on day or half-day tours, cross-border services or special services not included in timetables.

Cost: 3 days out of 8: IR£24 Adult, Family/Group* IR£22 per person. Children aged 3 to 15 at half price.
* To consist of a minimum of 5 adults (with 2 children counting as one adult) or husband & wife plus a child.

Purchase: From Bus Eireann sales offices throughout Ireland.

Dublin One Day Ticket

Availability: Available to anyone for unlimited travel on urban transport in Dublin and suburbs.

Coverage: Gives one day's travel on Dublin city buses and suburban trains (including DART services). Rail travel limits are Balbriggan, Kilcoole and Maynooth. Also available are 4-day Explorer Tickets and Family 1-day Tickets as well as family and individual one-day tickets valid for bus travel only.

Restrictions/Conditions of Use: Not valid on Airport or Ferryport motor coaches.

Cost: One Day Ticket (buses & trains) - IR£3.50, buses only IR£2.40; children 3-15 half price. 4-day Explorer Ticket IR£8. Family* 1-day ticket for all travel at IR£5.40 with bus only ticket at IR£4.50.
* Family to mean mother and/or father and up to four of their children under the age of 16.

Purchase: From city and suburban rail stations in the Dublin area, from Dublin Bus Booking Office in Upper O'Connell Street, from the Travel Centre in Abbey Street and from authorised ticket agents throughout the city.

ISRAEL

Israbus Pass

Availability/Coverage: Offers unlimited travel for 7, 14, 21 or 30 days on Egged bus routes throughout Israel. Allows discounts at a number of museums and restaurants, on car rental facilities and on Egged tours and services.

Cost: 7 days US$59m 14 days US$95, 21 days US$115, 30 days US$129.

Purchase: Available from all sales offices of Egged Tours including Ben Gurion Airport, Tel Aviv.

ITALY

Italian Tourist Tickets 🚋
(Biglietto Turistico di Libera Circolazione - BTLC)

Availability: Italian Tourist Tickets offer several facilites for rail travel to visitors to the country - that is anyone permanently residing outside Italy.

Travel at Will Tickets

Coverage: Gives 8, 15, 21 or 30 consecutive days unlimited travel in 1st or 2nd class on the Italian State Railways (FS) network. Includes seat reservation fees - if purchased in Italy - and fast train supplements within Italy.

Restrictions/Conditions of Use: Not available on private railways. 15, 21 and 30 day tickets may be extended at main Italian railway stations on payment of the appropriate extra fee. Passes must be validated by the issuing office or by an FS station before commencement of the first journey or by a ticket inspector on the train when crossing the Italian border; the ticket then becomes valid from that date. Passport number and proof of residence outside Italy required at time of purchase.

Cost: 8 days - 1st class £108, 2nd class £72; 15 days - 1st class £134, 2nd class £90; 21 days - 1st class £156, 2nd class £104, 30 days - 1st class £188, 2nd class £126 or equivalent in currency of country where purchased. Children aged 4-11 half price. Cost does not include service charge of - in the UK - £4 per pass.

Purchase: From CIT/Citalia sales offices worldwide, at international airports in Italy and at 20 principal Italian railway stations including frontier stations. Citalia address in the UK is 3-4 Lansdowne House, Croydon CR9 1LL; ☎081-686 0677, fax 081-686 0328, telex 8812133. Also available in the UK from Wasteels Travel at 121 Wilton Road, London SW1V 1JZ; ☎071-834 7066/071 834 6744, telex 266454. Sold in North America by post from Forsyth Travel Library whose address and telecommunication details can be found on page 96.

Flexi Card (Italy Flexi Railcard)

Coverage: Valid for 4 days travel within a specified period of 9 days, for 8 days out of 21 or for 12 days out of 30.

Similar conditions apply as for the Travel at Will ticket except that after validation the holder must enter the propsed daily journey on the ticket before the start of each day's trip.

Cost: 4 days travel out of 9 - £80 1st class, £54 2nd class; 8 days out of 21 - £118 1st class, £78 2nd class; 12 days out of 30 - £150 1st class, £100 2nd class.

Kilometric Tickets

Coverage: Valid for 2 months and allowing up to 20 trips for a total of 3,000 kilometres shared by up to 5 persons. The kilometric value of the ticket must be shared by the number of persons travelling, with children aged 4 to 11 qualifying for half the distance travelled on each trip, in effect paying half price. All tickets may be purchased up to 2 months before use and once validated (by issuing office/railway authorities) the pass must be used within its period of validation.

Except that the pass does not include fast train supplements, all other details as for Travel at Will tickets.

Cost: 1st class £125, 2nd class £73.

International Rail Passes valid in Italy:

All types of Eurail passes and InterRail Cards, Rail Europ Senior Cards.

City Transportation *U*

Many Italian cities offer half-day, one, two and three day tickets and weekly go-as-you-please tickets for visitors.

Samples:

ATAC in Rome produce a half-day ticket at L800 valid on their city services and a whole day ticket (BIG) covering the entire urban network of ATAC, FS and ACOTRAL public transport in the Rome area at L2800. Also available are "Circuito turistico" tickets at L6000, a weekly ticket at L10000 and a variety of one-monthly tickets. May be purchased from the ATAC information bureau in the Piazza dei Cinquecento and from sales outlets throughout the city.

ACTV in Venice offer 24-hour tickets at L10000 and 3-day tickets at L17000.

ATM in Milan have available a one-day ticket costing L3500 and a two-day ticket at L6000 with a weekly card at L10400.

JAPAN

Japan Rail Pass

Availability: Available to tourist visitors to Japan and to Japanese nationals permanently residing abroad or married to a national of an overseas country.

Coverage: Gives unlimited travel on the national railway system of Japan Railways Group (JR) and valid for 7, 14 or 21 days in Green (1st) or Ordinary (2nd) classes. Includes travel on Shinkansen super expresses, limited and ordinary expresses and local trains on all JR lines, on local services of JR bus companies, on the bus divisions of the Hokkaido, Shikoku & Kyushu railway companies and on some JR high speed bus lines as well as the JR ferry service Miyajima-Miyajimaguchi. Seat reservations may be made in advance without additional payment at a Travel Service Centre or Green Window (Midori-no-madoguchi) at most JR railway stations.

Restrictions/Conditions of Use: If an Ordinary pass is held and the holders wishes to use a berth or green car seat, regular berth or green car charges and associated limited or ordinary express charges must be paid. If a Green pass is held and a berth in a sleeping car train is required or the holder wishes to have Private Compartments on the Shinkansen or limited express "Super View ODORIKO", payment for a regular berth or Green Private Compartment and the associated Shinkansen, limited express or ordinary express fee must be made. Passport required at time of purchase.

Cost: Green (1st) class - 7 days ¥37,000; 14 days ¥60,000;, 21 days ¥78,000. Ordinary (2nd) class - 7 days ¥27,800, 14 days ¥44,200, 21 days ¥56,600. 50% reduction for children aged 6 to 11.

Purchase: The pass must be purchased through overseas offices of Japan Air Lines, Japan Travel Bureau, Nippon Travel Agency, Kinki Nippon Tourist or Tokyu Tourist Corporation who will issue an exchange order to be presented within three months at one of 25 JR Travel Service Centres in Japan including those in Tokyo, Yokohama, Sapporo, Nagoya, Kyoto, Osaka, Hiroshima and Shimonoseki as well as from the JR Information and Ticket Office at Tokyo-Narita Airport. In the UK the pass is available through Thomas Cook (**via Compass - details at foot of** page three).

Tokyo Area Transport Passes
🚋/U

Teito Rapid Transit Authority (Eidan)

A pass known as a **One Day Open Ticket** is available to anyone and gives unlimited travel on TRTA's metro system in Tokyo. When bought in advance it can be used any time within six months of purchase. *Cost:* ¥650 with half price for children aged 6 to 11; purchased from 114 of TRTA's stations for same day travel. Also available are a one-month pass costing ¥15,800, a 3-month pass ¥45,000 and a 6-month pass at ¥85,000. All tickets/passes can be bought in advance from 28 of Teito's metro station pass offices.

Toei Lines

Metro, bus and tram one day tickets cost ¥650

JR Inner-Tokyo Rail Tickets

One day tickets are priced ¥720.
Also available are combined one day JR/Tokunai-Toei rail-metro-bus-tram tickets at ¥1100 plus all-systems ticket at ¥1400.

Other railway and city transport reduced-rate tickets

Most major cities in Japan offer one-day and longer-period tickets suitable for overseas visitors. They range from one-day tram-only tickets in *Nagasaki & Hiroshima* (including the Miyajima ferry) at ¥500 & 840 respectively to a metro, bus and tram ticket in *Sapporo* at ¥830. Further examples of one-day travel offers are bus-only tickets in *Sendai* at ¥810 (¥540 for inner zone only), in *Yokohama* at ¥540, in *Kamakura* (Keikyu & Enoden buses only) at ¥630 and in *Fukuoka* at ¥500; bus/tram tickets in *Hakodate* at ¥900; metro/bus tickets in *Yokohama* at ¥830, in *Nagoya* (City Transport buses only) at ¥740, in *Kyoto* at ¥1050 and in *Osaka* at ¥800.

Railway reduced-rate ticket offers include JR "Hokkaido Free" and "Hokkaido Pair" (valid for 2 persons) tickets - covering bus services but not Seikan tunnel journeys - costing ¥33,400 ("HF") and ¥41,100 ("HP") in Ordinary class; JR Shikoku train & bus 5-day "Free Pass" at ¥15,400; JR Kyushu "Go-you ken" 1st class 3-day passes at ¥19,800 with 5-day passes at ¥29,700 (not valid on Shinkansen trains and on buses) and JR "Kyushu Ladies" passes; Nagano Electric Railway "Rail Fan Free" 2-day ticket at ¥2700; Nagoya Railroad "2 Day Free" ticket valid on trains and the monorail at ¥3300; Tobu Railway "Nikko Kinugawa Free Pass" (excludes express supplements) 4-day ticket at ¥5100; "Seishun (youth) 18 Tickets" composed of five tickets at ¥11,300, each of which is valid for unlimited travel on JR's Ordinary trains for one day during the periods Feb 20-Apr. 10, July 20-Sept. 10 and Dec. 10 - Jan. 20.

There are many other "wide", "new wide", "mini", "free", etc. travel-at-will tickets on JR, Kinki Nippon, Odakyu and Keihan Electric railways and the other railways of Japan.

AVAILABLE FROM THOMAS COOK

To fully plan your visit to Japan with timings of rail services and the routes which they follow we recommend the **Thomas Cook Overseas Timetable** and the **Thomas Cook World Rail Map**. Full details on page 94.

For details of obtaining the Thomas Cook Publishing sales leaflet and ordering the publications featured on this page refer to the footnote on page two.

LUXEMBOURG

Benelux Tourrail Card

Availability: Available to anyone for unlimited 1st or 2nd class travel over the lines of Luxembourg National Railways (Société Nationale des Chemins de Fer Luxembourgeois - CFL) for 5 days of travel within a specified 17-day period; also valid in Belgium and the Netherlands.

For all other details of the Benelux Tourrail Card and **Benelux-Weekend Return Ticket** refer to the section for Belgium.

Billet "Réseau"/Oeko-Billjee (Network Ticket)

Availability: Available to anyone for one day's unlimited travel on the public transport network of Luxembourg.

Coverage: Valid for 2nd class travel on the four major transport companies of Luxembourg - CFL, AVL, RGTR and TICE - operating rail and road services. Supplement payable for transfer to 1st class.

Cost: Lfr120. A book of 5 billets "réseau" (Carnet "réseau") costs Lfr480. Also on sale are billet "courte distance" for a specific one-hour journey at Lfr30, a book of 10 of these tickets costing Lfr240. A similar series of tickets for one month's travel are also available including a season ticket valid only on AVL bus services in Luxembourg City.

Purchase: One-day and one-hour tickets may be bought on board buses and all tickets can be purchased from ticket offices operated by the various transport companies, from railway stations and other appointed sales outlets.

International Rail Passes valid in Luxembourg: All types of Eurail passes and InterRail Cards, Rail Europ Senior Card (plus Benelux travel cards and tickets).

MALAYSIA

Malayan Railpass

Availability: Available to holders of passports other than Malaysian and Singaporean.

Coverage: Gives unlimited travel for 10 or 30 days on services of Keretapi Tanah Melayu (KTM) in Malaysia and on journeys to and from Singapore.

Restrictions/Conditions of Use: Passport needs to be produced.

Cost: 10 days US$40, 30 days US$85. 50% reduction for children aged 4 to 12.

Purchase: Sold at principal railway stations in Malaysia and in Singapore.

MOROCCO

Carte d'Abonnement V3

Availability: Available to anyone for unlimited travel on the rail network of Office National des Chemins de Fer (ONCF).

Coverage: Valid for one month in 1st or 2nd class on the services of Moroccan Railways, the cost depending on the distance travelled.

Restrictions/Conditions of Use: Not available on TNR trains (Trains navettes rapides).

Cost (in dirhams): Tanger-Rabat Dh996 1st class, Dh663 2nd class. Tanger to Casablanca (Port), Marrakech & Oujda and Casablanca-Oujda Dh1146 1st class, Dh767 2nd class. Meknes to Casablanca & Tanger Dh944 1st class, Dh629 2nd class. Tanger-Fes Dh1045 1st class, Dh697 2nd class. Casablanca to Marrakech Dh894 1st class, Dh596 2nd class. Casablanca-Rabat Dh552 1st class, Dh370 2nd class. Casablanca-Fes Dh1094 1st class, Dh731 2nd class. A "droit de garantie" supplement of Dh43.50 applies to each card. There are also cards for periods of 3 months, 6 months, 9 months and one year.

Purchase: Sold by sales offices of Moroccan Railways and from railway stations.

NETHERLANDS

Benelux Tourrail Card 🚃

Availability: Available to anyone for unlimited 1st or 2nd class travel for 5 days out of 17 on the services of Netherlands Railways (Nederlandse Spoorwegen - NS) and on the national railways of Belgium and Luxembourg. For full coverage and further details as well as information on the ***Benelux-Weekend Return Ticket*** refer to the section for Belgium.

Cost: Adult (26 +) 1st class £67, 2nd class £45; Youth (aged 4-25) 1st class £47, 2nd class £32.

Purchase: Obtainable from railway stat-

ions in the Netherlands and from Netherlands Railways sales offices and appointed agents worldwide - in the UK from their London office at 25/28 Buckingham Gate, London SW1E 6LD; passport necessary.

Holland Rail Pass

Availability: Available to anyone permanently residing outside Holland (the Netherlands).

Coverage: Valid for 1st or 2nd class travel on Netherlands Railways for any 3 days within a specified period of 15 consecutive days.

Cost: 1st class £31, 2nd class £25; accompanied children (maximum of 3) aged 4 to 11 £1 each.

Purchase: From railway stations in the Netherlands and from Netherlands Railways sales offices and authorised agents worldwide. Passport necessary.

Rover Tickets 🚃/🚌

Netherlands Railways offer a wide variety of Rover tickets for use on their services.
1-Day Rover
Entitles the holder to one (specified) day's unlimited travel on the NS network.
Cost: 1st class £24, 2nd class £16.
7-Day Rover
For unlimited NS rail travel on 7 consecutive days.
Cost: 1st class £54.50, 2nd class £36.50.
Public Transport Link Rover
Issued in conjunction with one and seven day Rovers and valid for the same period, allowing the holder to unlimited travel on all city and country buses and trams in the Netherlands and on the Amsterdam and

Rotterdam metro systems.
Cost: 1-day £2, 7-day £7

Teenage Rover
Available on the NS rail network in June, July and August for young persons uo to the age of 18 and giving unlimited 2nd class travel on any 4 days out of a specified period of 10 consecutive days.
Cost: £15

Teenage Rover Plus tickets offer the same facilities as the Teenage Rover but also include travel on buses, trams and the metro systems. *Cost:* £18.50.

Multi-Rover Tickets
Entitle 2 to 6 persons one day's (specified) unlimited rail travel with 2 children aged 4 to 11 counting as one passenger. Tickets can be used after 0900 Monday to Friday and all day on Saturday, Sunday and public holidays. In June, July and August they can be used at any time.
Cost: 1st class - 2 persons £35, 3 persons £44, 4 persons £49, 5 persons £54, 6 persons £59. 2nd class - 2 persons £24, 3 persons £29, 4 persons £33, 5 persons £36, 6 persons £38.

Railrunners (Children)

Children between 4 and 11 years of age pay 60% of the adult fare on NS trains and half the adult fare on the Dutch section of international journeys. However with Railrunner tickets children travelling with a fare-paying adult pay only £0.30 (30 pence) per child regardless of the length or class of the journey. Up to three children can travel on Railrunner tickets with any one adult.

International Rail Passes valid in the Netherlands: All types of Eurail pass and InterRail Cards, Rail Europ Senior Card. (plus Benelux travel cards and tickets).

Amsterdam - GVB *U*

Availability/Coverage: Available to visitors as 1-day or multiple-day tickets, Amsterdam Municipal Transport authorities (GVB) offer unlimited travel on their bus, tram and metro lines as well as urban rail services within the city.

Restrictions/Conditions of Use: Not available on services to and from Schiphol Airport.

Cost: 1 day Dfl.9.50, 2 days Dfl.12.60, 3 days Dfl.15.60, 4 days Dfl.18.50 and in multiples of Dfl.2.90 per day up to Dfl.33 for 9 days.

Purchase: The 1-day ticket may be purchased on trams and buses and in Metro stations. Tickets for 2 days or more are available from the GVB information and ticket office opposite Centraal Railway Station, at the GVB Central Office 'Scheepvaarthuis' in Prins Hendrikskade and from the GVB counter at Amstel Station.

NEW ZEALAND

New Zealand Travelpass (InterCity)

Availability: Available to anyone for journeys on the services of New Zealand Railways (InterCity).

Coverage: Gives unlimited travel for any 8 days out of a specified 14-day period, 15 days out of 22 or 22 days out of 31 on InterCity trains, coaches and Interislander Ferries. Also offers discounts at some hotels.

Cost: until June 30, 1991 - 8 days from 14 NZ$344; 15 days from 22 NZ$447; 22 days from 31 NZ$551.

From July 1, 1991 to June 30, 1992 - 8 days from 14 NZ$360; 15 days from 22 NZ$447, 22 days from 31 NZ$599. Half price for children aged 5 to 14.

Purchase: Obtainable from InterCity Travel Centres and accredited agents in New Zealand and from New Zealand Travel wholesalers and authorised agents worldwide. In the UK from Thomas Cook **(via Compass - details at foot of page three).**

Other reduced-rate facilities offered by InterCity include a 14 or 28 day Travel Card issued in association with the Youth Hostel Association costing NZ$75 for 14 days and NZ$99 for 28 days and giving the holder a 50% discount on all InterCity coach services (except sightseeing), trains and Interislander Ferries. Can only be bought within New Zealand.

The Downunder Coach Pass valid in New Zealand and Australia for combined Greyhound/Mount Cook Line travel is covered in detail in the section for Australia. *Cost in New Zealand dollars:* 9 days NZ$407 Adult/NZ$326 child (aged 4-14); 12 days NZ$487/389, 18 days NZ$618/495, 24 days NZ$776/621, 32 days NZ$1013/810, 45 days NZ$1282/1026.

Backpacker Pass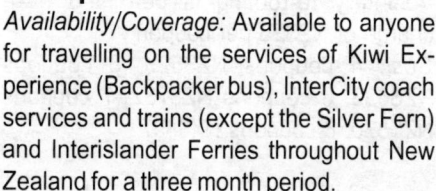

Availability/Coverage: Available to anyone for travelling on the services of Kiwi Experience (Backpacker bus), InterCity coach services and trains (except the Silver Fern) and Interislander Ferries throughout New Zealand for a three month period.

Cost: 10 vouchers NZ$309, 15 vouchers NZ$414, 20 vouchers NZ$519.

Purchase: Can be purchased from InterCity Travel Centres and accredited agents in New Zealand and outside New Zealand from international wholesalers and their agents, from Tourland Reisen Frankfurt in Germany, from Benns Rejser in Denmark, from National Australia Travel nationwide, NZTP Melbourne, Kirra Tours Adelaide and Australian NZCRO Queens-land in Australia.

Kiwi Coach Pass

Availability: Available to visitors to New Zeland for pre-paid motor coach travel.

Coverage: Valid for first class travel on the services of Mount Cook Landline and their associated companies throughout New Zealand. Also includes air travel across Cook Strait between Wellington & Nelson and Wellington & Blenheim, day trips to Waitomo Caves and Milford Sound and discounts of 10- 20% on services of Mount Cook Airlines and on a number of sight-seeing tours by ship, plane and road. Passes are valid for 7 days out of an 11-day period, 10 days out of 16, 15 days out of 23, 25 days out of 35 or 33 days out of 45.

Restrictions/Conditions of Use: Passes must be validated and travel completed within six months of the date of issue of the pass.

Cost: 7 days NZ$271, 10 days NZ$313, 15 days NZ$357, 25 days NZ$543, 33 days NZ$610. Children aged 4-14 half price; prices will increase by approx. 10-15%

from Oct. 1.

Purchase: Passes may be pre-purchased prior to arrival in New Zealand from Air New Zealand Travel Centres and their appointed agents worldwide who will issue a voucher or order which must be exchanged on arrival in New Zealand for the pass itself at a Mount Cook Line office in Auckland, Rotorua, Wellington or Christchurch.

Auckland - Day Rover 🚌

Availability: Available to anyone for unlimited travel on bus services operated by Auckland Regional Council in the Auckland area.

Restrictions/Conditions of Use: Valid after 0900 hours Monday to Friday and all day Saturday, Sunday and public holidays.

Cost: Adult NZ$8; children aged 4-14 at half price. Family passs for two adults and up to four children or one adult and up to five children NZ$12.
Also available are Ten-Trip Tickets offering savings of approximately 15% on ordinary single fares.

Purchase: Day rover tickets can be purchased from a number of stations in the Auckland Cityline area.

Wellington - Day Rover *U*

Availability: Available to anyone for unlimited travel on Cityline trains and road services in the Wellington region.

Coverage: Can also be used on the Kelburn Cable Car and Wellington City Transport buses.

Restrictions/Conditions of Use: Tickets are valid for travel between 0900 and 1600 and after 1800 hours Monday to Friday and all day at weekends and on public holidays.

Cost: Adult NZ$15; Family Ticket (valid for 2 adults and up to 4 children) NZ$30.
A similar Day Tripper ticket for 1 adult + 2 children is valid on scheduled WCT bus services and the Cable Car only and costs NZ$6.50.
WCT ten-trip tickets offering savings of approx. 20% on standard fares are also available.

Purchase: Day Rovers are sold at NZR Cityline stations. Day Tripper tickets may be purchased at the Cable Car and on board buses.

The New Zealand Airpass (Ansett New Zealand) ✈

Availability: Passes are available to persons permanently residing outside New Zealand travelling on international flights to and from New Zealand.

Coverage: A minimum of 4 and maximum of 8 coupons give unlimited travel on Ansett New Zealand's domestic services in economy class for a maximum stay of 60 days.

Restrictions/Conditions of Use: Any stopover/transit point constitutes one coupon. Voluntary re-routing is permitted at a charge of NZ$25 per coupon.
Cost: 4 coupons NZ$523, 5 coupons NZ$633, 6 coupons NZ$732, 7 coupons NZ$820, 8 coupons NZ$897

Purchase: From Ansett New Zealand sales offices worldwide and their appointed agents. Sales in New Zealand are limited to Ansett New Zealand offices and are subject to production of international travel tickets to and from New Zealand and evidence of overseas residency and are liable to a Goods and Services Tax.

Ansett New Zealand also offer a *Discover New Zealand Fare* which gives a 20% discount on ordinary economy class fares and a *See New Zealand Fare* offering a 30% discount.

Kiwi Air Pass (Mount Cook Airline) ✈

Availability: Available to visitors to New Zealand for travel on the services of Mount Cook Airline.

Coverage: The Kiwi Air Pass permits travel on the Mount Cook Airline scheduled network once in each direction on each sector of flight (with the exception of Milford Sound).

Restrictions/Conditions of Use: Travel must be completed within 30 days of tickets becoming valid.

Cost: Up to Sept. 30 - Adult NZ$809; child (under 15 years of age) NZ$605.
From Oct. 1 - Adult NZ$856; child NZ$643

Purchase: A voucher or order can be purchased outside New Zealand from sales offices of Air New Zealand and their authorised agents and the pass validated and exchanged for tickets on arrival in New Zealand from a Mount Cook Line Travel Centre or Airport Office in Auckland, Rotorua, Wellington, Christchurch or Queenstown.

NORWAY

Nordturist Ticket 🚃 ⛴

Availability: Available to anyone resident outside Scandinavia for unlimited 1st or 2nd class travel on the national railways (NSB in Norway) and some ferry and bus services in Denmark, Finland, Norway and Sweden for 21 days.

Coverage: Also valid for travel on the NSB bus service Trondheim-Storlien, on the combined boat/bus route Halden/Sarpsborg - Strömstad as well as the Fred Olsen/KDS ferry service Kristiansand-Hirtshals; reductions of 50% on the DFDS Oslo-Copenhagen ferry, on the Larvik-Frederikshavn Line, on the Flåm-Bergen and other "Fylkesbaatane" routes, on the Bodö-Fauske-Narvik-Kirkenes North Norway bus route and on local bus and boat lines in Nordland. Free entrance to Hamar railway museum.

For cost and all other details regarding the pass refer to the section for Denmark.

International Rail Passes valid in Norway: All types of Eurail passes and InterRail Cards, Rail Europ Senior Card, Nordturist Ticket.

Oslo Card (Oslo-Kortet) *U*

Availability: Available to anyone for unlimited travel on public transport services in the Greater Oslo traffic area.

Coverage: Valid for 24, 48 or 72 hours on Oslo Public Transport Ltd. (AS Oslo Sporveier) tram, bus, underground railway, train and ferry services, on NSB suburban trains within Oslo and on all public transport in the four Greater Oslo travel zones. Also affords free entry to a number of museums and tourist attractions in the city; discounts on boat and coach sightseeing trips, theatre, cinema & opera tickets, the Tusenfryd Amusement Park, restaurants & shops, tourist train, car & ski rental as well as free parking at all municipal car parks. 30% discount on a return rail journey (adults only) by NSB services between stations within Norway and Oslo when rail tickets are purchased at the same time as a 3-day Oslo Card.

Restrictions/Conditions of Use: The rail discount/3-day Oslo Card offer is only available only at an NSB travel agency outside Oslo.

Cost: 1-day (24-hour) Card NoK90; 2- day (48-hour) Card NoK120; 3-day (72-hour) Card NoK160. Children aged 4-14 half price.

Purchase: From tourist information offices at Oslo Sentral Station and City Hall, from a number of city centre hotels and from camping sites in the Oslo area, from "Trafikanten" in Jernbanetorget, from Narvesen kiosks in the centre of Oslo, from most NSB sales agencies throughout Norway and from some passenger ships calling at Oslo.

Travel Passes in Oslo (Oslo Public Transport Ltd.) *U*

Visitors to Oslo can take advantage of special offers by Oslo Public Transport Ltd. (AS Oslo Sporveier) on their metro, tram, local train, bus and boat services within the city boundaries.

24-hour ticket costs NoK40 and can be bought from the "Trafikanten" information centre, from AS Oslo Sporveier ticket offices, from manned metro stations, from post offices, Narvesen kiosks and the City Hall information centre. Children aged 4-15 at half price.

7-day ticket costs NoK130 and may be purchased from same outlets as the 24-hour ticket plus manned railway stations in Oslo. Young people aged 4-17 at half price.

Also available are *Flexi cards* offering 8 city rides within one hour and sold by the same outlets as the 7-day ticket as well as on board vehicles.

Visit Norway Pass (Braathens SAFE) ✈

Availability: Available only to permanent residents of countries outside Scandinavia.

Coverage: Valid for a month on Braathens domestic services within Norway and the journey must commence between May 1 and Sept. 30. For purposes of the pass, Norway is split into North and South Zones with the "border" city being Trondheim and so-called *short* journeys are permitted within each zone with a *long* journey allowing travel between the two zones.

Restrictions/Conditions of Use: Each journey must cover cover the shortest possible distance between commencing point and destination with no stopovers allowed en route. Proof of residence in the form of a valid passport may be requested during travel in Norway.

Cost: Short journey pass - £36/US$57. Long journey pass - £72/US$114. Children aged 2 to 12 get a 50% discount.

Purchase: Outside Norway, passes may be purchased from airlines which have an interline agreement with Braathens SAFE and from their authorised agents; if a final itinerary has not been finalised, a ticket order will be issued and on arrival in Norway will be exchange for Visit Norway Pass tickets.

PAPUA NEW GUINEA

Visit Papua New Guinea (Air Niugini) ✈

Availability: Available to persons who are bona fide residents of any country other than Papua New Guinea, the Solomon Islands and Irian Jaya (Indonesia) and whose international travel to and from Papua New Guinea is by Air Niugini.

Coverage: Valid for a minimum stay of 5 days and maximum of 30 days on domestic Air Niugini routes in economy class. Minimum of 4 flight coupons with no limit to the number of additional coupons.

Restrictions/Conditions of Use: A maximum of two transfers are permitted - at Port Moresby and Lae only. Proof of holder's residency outside Papua New Guinea or the holding of international travel tickets must be available during travel.

Cost: 4 flight coupons - US$299; each additional coupon US$50.

Purchase: Tickets must be purchased outside Papua New Guinea from sales offices of Air Niugini and their appointed agents.

PERU

Visit Peru Airpasses (Faucett) ✈

Availability: Persons resident outside Peru who must be holding international travel tickets as indicated against each pass.

Coverage: For travel on Compania de Aviacion Faucett domestic services through Peru.

Unlimited 60-Day Peru Airpass
Can be used once to each point served by Faucett Airlines except Lima which can be used as a connecting point as many times as necessary. Holders must arrive in Lima on a Faucett flight from Miami.
Cost: US$180
Unlimited 60-Day Peru Airpass
Same conditions as above except that

holders can arrive in Lima on any international carrier.

Cost: US$250

4-Coupons 60-Day Peru Airpass

Four coupons good for four single flights or two round trips. Holders must arrive on Lima on any international carrier.

Cost: US$180; extra coupons are available at US$30 each.

Purchase: May be bought from Faucett sales offices outside Peru and their appointed agents.

POLAND

Polrailpass 🚃

Availability: Available to anyone for unlimited travel on Polish State Railways (PKP) system.

Coverage: Journeys in 1st or 2nd class for 8, 15 and 21 days or one month.

Cost: 8 days - 1st class US$50, 2nd class US$35; 15 days - 1st class US$60, 2nd class US$40; 21 days - 1st class US$67, 2nd class US$45; 1 month - 1st class US$75, 2nd class US$50. Children 4-10 years at half price.

Purchase: From Polorbis travel offices in London and Cologne and from Orbis in New York; also from the following sales agents - Reser in Stockholm, Transtours in Paris, Vindrose in Copenhagen, Chrobot Reisen in Zürich, Kennedy Travel Bureau in Toronto and Durch in Vienna.

International Rail Passes valid in Poland: InterRail Cards, EastRail Pass and European East Pass.

PORTUGAL

Tourist Ticket (Bilhete Turistico) 🚃

Availability: Available to anyone for unlimited travel on the Portuguese Railways (CP) network.

Coverage: Valid for 7, 14 or 21 days in 1st or 2nd class on the services of Caminhos de Ferro Portugueses.

Cost: 7 days - Esc15,200, 14 days - Esc24,200, 21 days - Esc34,600. Children aged 4 to 11 half price; proof of age may be required..

Purchase: Obtainable from CP stations and sales offices in Portugal and at TAP-Air Portugal offices worldwide if purchased at the same time as an air ticket.

International Rail Passes valid in Portugal: All types of Eurail passes, InterRail Card (under 26 only), Rail Europ Senior Card.

Passes Sociais & Passe Turistico *U*

Passes Sociais

Availability: Available to anyone for travel in Lisbon and its suburbs on services of Companhia Carris de Ferro de Lisboa, the Metro, Rodoviária Nacional, Transtejo, CP and Transportes dos S.M. do Barreiro.

Coverage: One month passes give unlimited travel on trams, buses, underground railway (Metro), suburban trains and Tagus Ferry. The cost depends on the number of zones in which travel around

Lisbon and the outer suburbs is permitted and there are versions for senior citizens which carry time restrictions on Monday to Friday travel. There are also passes for travel within the three outer zones only.

Cost: L Pass valid only on Carris & Metro services Esc2645; L-1 Lisbon + outer zone 1 Esc3510; L-1-2 Esc4215; L-1-2-3 Esc4775; Passe Carris valid on Carris services and including Algés-C. Quebrada Esc 3415. Reduced rates for children aged 4 to 12.

Passe Turistico

The Lisbon Tourist Pass for overseas visitors to the city has 4 and 7 day versions and is valid on Carris trams and buses and Metro routes within Lisbon.
Cost: 4 days Esc1100, 7 days Esc1550; passport and signature required at time of purchase.

Purchase (of all passes): From Carris sales offices and their authorised agents in Lisbon.

SINGAPORE

Singapore Explorer

Singapore Bus Service issues a ride-at-will ticket offering unlimited travel for one or three (consecutive) days on SBS and Trans-Island (TIBS) buses; also offers discounts at a number of places of interest in Singapore.
Cost: 1-day S$5, 3-day S$12.
Explorer tickets are of the scratch-and-ride variety and can be purchased at Singapore Airport, from major hotels, from the SBS Passenger Relations Centre and from authorised agents.

Malayan Railpass

Available for rail travel by overseas visitors between Malaysia and Singapore and vice versa; may be purchased in Singapore. Cost and details can be found under the section for Malaysia.

SPAIN

Tarjeta Turistica (Tourist Pass)

Marketed in North America as the Spain Railpass; also available is a Flexipass.
Availability: Available to anyone residing outside Spain for travel on the services of the Spanish National Railways (RENFE).

Coverage: Valid for unlimited travel in 1st or 2nd class for 8, 15 or 22 consecutive days travel on scheduled RENFE and on international trains throughout Spain except as listed under "*Restrictions*". 8 and 15 day Railpasses are sold in North America as well as Flexipasses for any 4 days travel out of 15.

Restrictions/Conditions of Use: Passport required at time of purchase plus proof of residence outside Spain for Spanish nationals. Travel is not permitted on the Paris-Madrid and the Barcelona-Zürich Talgo trains. Reservation fees are payable as are fast train and sleeper supplements but holders of 1st class tourist cards are exempt from paying 2nd class couchette supplements on RENFE domestic trains. Booking in advance is strongly recommended. The pass must be dated at a RENFE station or office before commencement of the first journey.

Cost (Prices are subject to confirmation): 8 days - 1st class US$165, 2nd class US$120; 15 days - 1st class US$265, 2nd class US$190; 22 days - 1st class US$320, 2nd class US$245; 50% reduction for children aged 4 to 11. Spain Railpass prices in the USA vary slightly from these rates; cost of the 4-days-in-15 Flexipass is US$109 1st class and US$83 2nd class.

Purchase: In Spain from RENFE travel offices and from railway stations in Barcelona (Sants), Madrid, Irun & Port Bou, from the RENFE offices in Paris (1 Avenue Marceau) and Buenos Aires, from main European railway stations (BR Victoria Station in London) and from other appointed sales agents in South America and Europe including - in London - from Wasteels Travel at 121 Wilton Road, London SW1V 1JZ; ☎ 071-834 7066/828 5949, telex 266454. In North America passes may be purchased from Donna Brunstad Associates in Westport - Connecticut, from Rail Europe/French Rail Inc. at White Plains - New York and by post from Forsyth Travel Library whose address and telecommunication details are on page 96.

Other types of passes issued by RENFE include the ***Tarjeta Familiar Nacional*** available to those persons already holding a family type pass in their own country and which gives up to 50% discount on adult fares and up to 75% on childrens' fares and the ***Tarjeta Joven Nacional*** youth pass allowing holders (aged 12 to 26) of a national youth pass in their own country discounts for travel by RENFE.

International Rail Passes valid in Spain:
All types of Eurail passes, InterRail Card (-26 only) and the Rail Europ Senior Card.

SWEDEN

Nordturist Ticket 🚃 🚢

Availability: Available to anyone resident outside Scandinavia for unlimited 1st or 2nd class travel on Swedish National Railways (SJ), national railways of the other Scandinavian countries and some bus and boat services for a period of 21 days.

Coverage: Also valid on Stockholm-Turku Silja Line ferries, Göteborg-Frederikshavn Stena Line ships, SJ ferries Helsingborg-Helsingør & Trelleborg-Sassnitz and the bus/ferry route Strömstad-Sarpsborg/Halden; 50% reductions on Gotland ferries Nynäshamn-Visby & Oskarshamn-Visby, on Silja Line Stockholm-Helsinki services, on TT Line Trelleborg-Travemünde and Umeå-Vaasa ships, on Växjo-Hultsfred-Västervik railway. Also allows free entry to the railway museum at Gävle and reductions on Stockholm-Mariehamn Birka Cruises.

Cost: Adult (26 +) - 1st class SeK2180, 2nd class SeK1625; youth (aged 12-25) - 1st class SeK1635, 2nd class SeK1215; children (aged 4-11) - 1st class SeK815, 2nd class SeK 1090.

For all other details refer to the section for Denmark.

Inlandsbanan Pass

Details not available at time of going to press; pass may not be available in 1991.

International Rail Passes valid in Sweden: All types of Eurail passes and InterRail Cards, Rail Europ Senior Card, Nordturist Ticket.

SL Tourist Card - Stockholm
U

Availability: Available to anyone for 24 or 72 hours unlimited travel on Storstockholms Lokaltrafik (SL) services.

Coverage: Valid on SL suburban trains, the metro system and buses in the county of Stockholm (except the Arlanda Airport bus) and on Djurgården ferries; also permits free entry to the transport museum. The 72-hour card gives free access to several other places of interest.

Cost: 24-hours SeK30 (central area + Djurgården ferries); SeK55 for card extending coverage to suburban services. 72 hours (3 days) SeK105 for city and suburban services. 50% reduction for young persons under the age of 18. There is also a monthly ticket valid for one calendar month.

Purchase: From the SL Center at T-Centralen metro station (Sergels Torg), from Stockholm City Tourist Office and from Pressbyrån kiosks.

Stockholm Card *U*

Availability: Available to anyone for unlimited travel on public transport services in the city for 24, 48 or 72 hours.

Coverage: Valid on Stockholm's train, metro and bus services, permits free travel on the "Tourist Line" city sightseeing tour and Strömma Kanal trip, free car parking facilities and admittance to a number of museums, the palaces which are open to the public and other places of interest, round trip by boat to Drottningholm Palace for the price of a one-way journey.

Cost: 24 hours - SeK125; 48 hours (2 days) - SeK250; 72 hours (3 days) - SeK375. 2 children per adult travel free.

Purchase: From Sweden House tourist centre, from Hotel Centralen, from the Central Railway Station and the SL-Center at T-Centralen metro station (Sergels Torg), from the tourist information desk at City Hall (summer only), from Kaknaes Tower and from more than 100 Pressbyrån news kiosks.

Gothenburg City Passes *U*

Göteborgs Spårvägar (Gothenburg Transport) issue a 24-hour pass (24-Timmarskortet) valid for unlimited travel on their bus and tram services within the city and

Styrsöbolaget ferries. At weekends and on public holidays the pass is valid for three persons - the holder plus two young people under the age of 17.
Cost: SeK27.
A Reduced Rate Card (Rabattkortet) valid for one year at SeK350 entitles the holder to purchase other cards including Low-Price Passes (Lågpriskortet) valid for one month and a Monthly Pass (Månads-kortet).

SWITZERLAND

Swiss Pass & Swiss Flexi Pass

Availability: Available to persons permanently resident outside Switzerland and Liechtenstein for unlimited 1st or 2nd class journeys on the Swiss Travel System.

Coverage: The Swiss Pass is valid for 4, 8 or 15 days or for 1 month and the Flexi Pass for 3 days travel within a specified period of 15 days on Swiss Federal Railways services (SBB/CFF/FFS), on a number of private railways, lake steamers and buses and also gives reductions on many mountain railways and funiculars. In addition unlimited travel is permitted on buses and trams in the following towns:
Aarau, Baden & Wettingen, Basel, Bern, Biel (Bienne), Fribourg, Genève, La Chaux-de-Fonds, Lausanne, Locarno, Lugano, Luzern, Neuchâtel, Olten, St. Gallen, Schaffhausen, Solothurn, Thun, Vevey & Montreux, Winterthur, Zug and Zürich. Passes are issued with a synoptic map.

Cost: **Swiss Pass** 4 days - 1st class Sfr270/£108; 2nd class Sfr180/£72. Not

available in North America.
8 days - 1st class Sfr320/£128/US$239; 2nd class Sfr220/£88/US$159.
15 days - 1st class Sfr380/£152/US$289; 2nd class Sfr260/£104/US$189.
1 month - 1st class Sfr520/£208/US$398; 2nd class Sfr360/£144/US$269.
Swiss Flexi Pass (3 days out of 15) - 1st class Sfr270/£108/US$199; 2nd class Sfr180/£72/US$129.
Children aged 6-15 at half price (refer to *Swiss Family Card* note.

Purchase: From the Swiss National Tourist Offices or offices of Swissair in Amsterdam, Brussels, Düsseldorf, Frankfurt/Main, Hamburg, London, Madrid, Milan, Munich, Paris, Rome, Stockholm, Stuttgart and Vienna, Cairo, Chicago, Johannesburg, Los Angeles, New York, San Francisco and Toronto (information only in Buenos Aires, Sydney-Edgecliff, Tel Aviv and Tokyo) and from appointed agents worldwide. May also be purchased at Geneva & Zürich airports and at Swiss frontier railway stations. Additionally in the USA from Rail Europe/French Rail Inc. in White Plains, New York State and by mail order from Forsyth Travel Library whose address and telecommunication details appear on page 96.
Passport or identity card required at time of purchase.

Swiss Half-Fare Card

Availability: 1-year card is available to anyone; one-month card to persons residing outside Switzerland and Liechtenstein.

Coverage: The holder can buy tickets at half the ordinary advertised fare for travel on the Swiss Travel System.

EUROTRAIN

DISCOUNT RAIL FARES FOR THE UNDER 26s

Choose the route to suit you from any UK station
Tickets valid 2 months - Stop off anywhere en route
Ferry crossing included

	o/w from	rtn from		o/w from	rtn from
■ Amsterdam	£25.30	£48.30	■ Paris	£31.50	£57.80
■ Berlin	£61.00	£97.90	■ Cologne	£35.00	£62.90
■ Brussels	£25.00	£43.00	■ Rome	£84.20	£167.00

EXPLORE THE EAST WITH EUROTRAIN EXPLORER PASSES

ONE WEEK'S UNLIMITED TRAVEL IN

*HUNGARY OR CZECHOSLOVAKIA
FROM ONLY £18.50
*POLAND FROM ONLY £13.00

* ALSO AVAILABLE FOR FULL TIME
STUDENTS OF ANY AGE

SEE THE CONTINENT WITH OUR BARGAIN EXPLORERS:

● **EASTERN EUROPE EXPLORER - FROM £182.50**
London-Amsterdam-Berlin-Prague-Budapest-Vienna-Zurich-Strasbourg-Luxembourg-Brussels-London

● **CAPITAL EXPLORER - FROM £80.00**
London-Paris-Brussels-Amsterdam-London...........................AND MANY MORE!

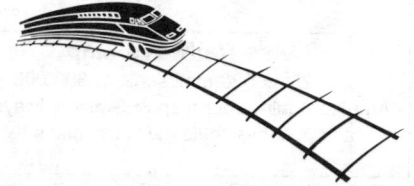

CALL 071 730 3402

OR VISIT
YOUR LOCAL
EUROTRAIN AGENT
OR
STUDENT TRAVEL SHOP

Restrictions/Conditions of Use: A passport or identity card number is required for the one-month card and a passport-type photograph for the 12-months card.

Cost: 1-year Card Sfr120*; 1-month Card Sfr75*
* *Refer to Swiss Family Card note.*

Purchase: From similar sales outlets to the Swiss Pass but not those in the USA.

Swiss Transfer Ticket
Offers visitors to Switzerland a one-day transfer by rail from airport or frontier station to any destination in Switzerland and vice versa.
Cost: Sfr120/£48 in 1st class, Sfr80/£32 in 2nd class; refer to *Swiss Family Card* note.
Purchase: Cannot be bought in Switzerland but only from some branches of the Swiss National Tourist Office (and their authorised agents) outside Switzerland.

Swiss Card
Gives the facilites offered under "Half-Fare Card" together with those of "Swiss Transfer Ticket" and is valid for 1 month. Issued with a synoptic map.
Cost: Adult - 1st class Sfr140/£56/US$109; 2nd class Sfr110/£44/US$79. Children (aged 6 to 15) 1st class Sfr85/£34; 2nd class Sfr55/£22. Refer to *Swiss Family Card* note.
Purchase: As for the Swiss Pass.

Swiss Family Card
Available for children aged 6 to 15 and unmarried young persons aged 16 to 25 when accompanied by one or both parents; children travel free and young people

at half price. The card is issued free.

Other reduced-rate offers by the Swiss Travel System include "Fly-Rail Baggage" and 10% reductions on the hire of ski-ing equipment. In North America Forsyth Travel Library and Rail Europe/French Rail Inc. offer Swiss Rail'n Drive Passes.

International Rail Passes valid in Switzerland: All types of Eurail passes and InterRail Cards, Rail Europ Senior Card.

Regional Pass 🚃 ⛴ 🚌

Availability: Available to anyone for unlimited or half price travel in 8 Swiss regions by rail, boat and post bus for 7 or 15 consecutive days. 7-day passes give unlimited travel for any 3 days (2 days in Region 4) and 50% reduction on remaining days; unlimited travel on all days in Regions 5, 7 & 8 (except on the Monte Brè bus in Region 8). 15-day passes offer unlimited travel for any 5 days and 50% reductions on remaining 10 days. On some services a reduction of 25% or 50% applies on all days of validity. Some passes give further reductions to holders of Swiss Passes, Swiss Cards and Half-Fare Cards.

Cost in Swiss Francs: Region	Validity	Period of issue*	1st class	2nd class	2nd class rail/ 1st class boat
1 - Montreux/Vevey	7 days	From April 1	78	—	66
2 - Chablais Region	7 days	From May 1	—	45	—
3 - Bernese Oberland	15 days	From May 1	160	125	135
4 - Central Switzerland	15 days	From April 1	—	140	158
- Central Switzerland	7 days	From April 1	¤	¤	¤
5 - Churfirsten/Säntis	7 days	From June 1	—	60	—
6 - Grisons (Graubünden)	15 days	From May 1	160	100	—
7 - Locarno/Ascona Region	7 days	From March 1	70	—	—
8 - Lugano Region	7 days	From March 1	70	—	—

Children aged 6 to 15 at half price. * *Terminating date for all tickets is Oct. 31.*

¤ - *This pass is available only to holders of the Swiss Pass, Swiss Card or Swiss Half-Fare Card (also a General Season Ticket); there is a 20% reduction in the prices of all Regional Passes to holders of these four passes.*

Purchase: Should be purchased from railway stations in the respective regions; a limited selection of regional passes is held by the Swiss National Tourist Office in London.

Swiss Boat Pass ⛴

Availability: Issued on behalf of fifteen Swiss shipping companies by the Association of Swiss Navigation Companies (VSSU), it allows unlimited travel at half price on regular advertised services operating on most of the major Swiss lakes and rivers during the period March 1 - Oct. 31 (in 1992 valid from April).

Coverage: Valid on ships of the following companies:

Compagnie Générale de Navigation sur Le Lac Léman (CGN) - sailings on Lake Geneva.

Société de Navigation sur Les Lacs de Neuchâtel et Morat SA - runs services on Lakes Neuchâtel, Morat and Bienne.

Bielersee-Schiffahrts-Gesellschaft (BSG) operates on Lake Biel (Bienne).

Basler Personen-Schiffahrts-Gesellschaft AG operate Rhine sailings.

Thuner- und Brienzersee Schiffsbetrieb BLS have 18 ships cruising daily on Lakes Thun & Brienz.

Schiffahrtsgesellschaft des Hallwilersees (SGH) on the Lake of Hallwil.

Schiffahrtsgesellschaft des Vierwaldstättersee (SGV) sail the famous paddle steamers on Lake Lucerne.

Schiffahrtsgesellschaft für den Zugersee (SGZ) run evening cruises on Lake Zug.

Zürichsee-Schiff-fahrtsgesellschaft (ZSG) are the company operating cruises on the

Lake of Zürich.

Zürichsee-Fähre Horgen-Meilen run the Horgen-Meilen car ferry on the Lake of Zürich.

Schiffahrtsgenossenschaft Greifensee (SGG) are the main Greifensee operators.

Schweizerische Schiffahrtsgesellschaft Untersee und Rhein have ships on the Rhine between Schaffhausen and Stein as well as on the Untersee lake.

Bodensee-Flotte SBB run the Swiss services on the "international" Lake Constance (Bodensee).

Navigazione Lago Maggiore operate from Locarno and Stresa on Lake Maggiore to Luino, Cannobio and Verbania-Intra and also call at the Brissago and Borromean Islands.

Società Navigazione del Lago di Lugano offer a choice of 50 boat trips on Lake Lugano.

A synoptic map of the different companies and their services is included with the pass

Restrictions/Conditions of Use: Personal details including passport number and signature must be entered on the pass by the holder and passport or identity card must be carried. The pass is not valid on special cruises and a supplement may be required on certain ships (e.g. 'Wilhelm Tell Express').

Cost: Sfr30

Purchase: From some Swiss National Tourist Offices, from sales offices of the participating shipping companies and their authorised agents, from the Automobile and Touring Club of Switzerland and from some local tourist offices in Switzerland.

City Transport Reduced-Rate Tickets

Most of the larger Swiss cities have runabout tickets on their public transport services; as an example *Geneva's* Transports Publics Genevois (TPG) offer 1-day tickets at Sfr8, 2-day at Sfr14 and 3-day at Sfr 18. One-day tickets are sold by sales agents throughout the city and the other tickets from the TPG stations at Cornavin and Rive.

TAHITI

Air Tahiti Passes ✈

For visitors to Tahiti, Air Tahiti issue three air travel passes:

1 - *Pass Leeward/Windward islands*
Covers travel to Moorea, Huahine, Raiatea and Bora-Bora and costs CFP29,000

2 - *Pass Leeward/Windward and Tuamotu Island*
As above then returning to Papeete via Rangiroa & Manihi. Cost CFP43,500

3 - *Pass Leeward/Windward and Tuamotu Island*
To and from Leeward/Windward Islands then to and from Tuamotu Islands (Rangiroa & Manihi). Cost CFP48,500

Restrictions/Conditions of Use: All travel must be by domestic services of Air Tahiti and Air Moorea and start and end at Papeete. One stopover allowed per island. Validity 28 days.

Purchase: From sales offices of Air Tahiti and their authorised agents.

THAILAND

Visit Thailand Rail Pass

Availability: Available to visitors holding passports other than Thai passports for travel on all State Railway of Thailand trains.

Coverage: The Red Pass is valid in 2nd and 3rd class travel and includes all supplementary charges such as air-conditioning and travel by Express trains. The Blue Pass is valid for 2nd & 3rd class travel on SRT trains but does not include supplementary charges.

Cost: Red Pass Bahts3000; Blue Pass Bahts1500. Children aged 3 to 12 and less than 150 centimetres in height travel at half fare.

Purchase: Obtainable from the Advance Booking Office at Bangkok Main Station (Hualampong), from railway stations at Padang Basar (Thai-Malaysian border), Hadd(Hat) Yai, Surat Thani and Chiang Mai and from SRT authorised ticket agencies.

Joint Ticket

Joint tickets are available to visitors to Thailand for specific journeys to places of interest. The ticket is valid for a combination of train and motor coach travel and, in some cases, on boat journeys. Joint tickets are on offer for the following journeys:

Bangkok-Phuket by train and coach.
Bangkok-Krabi by train and coach.
Bangkok-Phi Phi Island via Krabi or Phuket by train, coach and express boat service*

Bangkok-Koh Samui by train, coach and express boat or ferry.
Bangkok-Koh Pha Ngan by train, coach and express boat.
Bangkok-Chiang Rai via Chiang Mai by train and coach*
* *Breaks of journey can be made in Krabi, Phuket or Chiang Mai.*
Cost and further information on these tickets from the Advance Booking Centre at Hualampong Station in Bangkok (☎ (2) 2233762/2247788, fax (2) 2256068, telex 72242 TH).

TUNISIA

Carte Bleue

May be used by visitors to Tunisia for travel in Gran-Confort, 1st or 2nd class on the lines of Société Nationale des Chemins de Fer Tunisiens (SNCFT) for 7, 15 or 21 days.
Cost: 7 days - Confort class D40, 1st class D35, 2nd class D25. 15 days - Confort class D75, 1st class D65, 2nd class D45. 21 days - Confort class D110, 1st class D95, 2nd class D65. Supplement of 0.2 Dinars for travelling on trains which have supplementary charges for air-conditioning.

Other reduced-rate tickets on Tunisian Railways
Carte Tunisie Vacances offers 2nd class travel for 15 days for young persons aged 10 to 21 and all students up to the age of 28 and is valid only during school holiday periods. Cost D22 with supplement as above of 0.2 dinars.
Carte Jeune gives travel over a period of one year to the same category of persons as the Carte Tunisie Vacances with 50%

reductions during "white" periods of travel on SNCFT and 25% reduction in "yellow" periods of Tunisian Railways' travel calendar. Cost D5.5

For all the above tickets a passport must be produced and for the young persons' tickets proof of age and/or full time studies will be required.

Tickets must be purchased in Tunisia from sales offices of SNCFT and their appointed agents.

UNITED KINGDOM

(Including Northern Ireland, Jersey and the Isle of Man)

International Rail Passes valid in the United Kingdom: InterRail Cards, Rail Europ Senior Card.

BritRail Pass & BritRail Flexipass 🚋

Availability: Available to persons permanently resident outside the United Kingdom for unlimited travel on British Rail services.

Coverage: The BritRail Pass allows 1st class (Gold Pass) or standard class (Silver Pass) travel for 8, 15 or 22 consecutive days or one month on all scheduled British Rail trains in England, Scotland and Wales.
The BritRail Flexipass offers Gold Passes for adults and senior citizens and Silver Passes for adults, senior citizens and young people for any 4 days in a specified 8-day period, any 8 days out of 15 days or any 15 days in one month (15 days out of 2 months if qualified for the Youth fare).

Restrictions/Conditions of Use: A valid passport may be required at time of purchase and when using the pass plus proof of age for youth and senior citizen passes. The BritRail pass becomes valid when the first and last dates of travel are stamped on the pass by BR authorities at a British Rail station or travel centre and this must be done within six months of the date of purchase.

Purchase: Available from British Rail sales offices or appointed agents outside the UK. A pass coupon issued overseas can be exchanged for a pass at BR offices at Gatwick and Heathrow airports, at the British Travel Centre in Regent Street, London and at a number of other exchange points. In North America the pass is sold by BritRail Travel International Inc. in New York (1500 Broadway), Toronto and Vancouver and by post from Forsyth Travel Library whose address and telecommunication details appear on page 96.

Further offers available in North America include the BritFrance Pass (details under the section for France) and the BritRail/ Drive facility which combines a BritRail Flexipass with Hertz car rental and which is also available in other countries outside Europe. Details of the *London Extra* and *London Visitor Travelcard* offers can be found in the England section.

Cost: (in US dollars) Gold = 1st class; Silver = Standard (previously 2nd) class

BritRail Pass	Adult		Senior Citizen (60 +)		Youth (16-25)
	Gold	Silver	Gold	Silver	Silver
8 days	319	209	289	189	169
15 days	479	319	429	289	255
22 days	599	399	539	359	319
1 Month	689	456	619	419	375
Flexipass					
Any 4 days in 8	269	179	239	159	145
Any 8 days in 15	379	255	339	229	199
Any 15 days in 1 month	549	369	495	329	—
Any 15 days in 2 months	—	—	—	—	295

British Rail All Line Rover

Availability: Available to anyone for unlimited travel on British Rail scheduled services.

Coverage: Provides 7 or 14 days travel in first or standard class on BR's network in England, Wales and Scotland and on Wightlink's Portsmouth-Ryde and Lymington-Yarmouth ferries to the Isle of Wight plus 20% reduction on Windermere Iron Steam-boat sailings and 10% discount on the Keighley & Worth Valley Railway.

Restrictions/Conditions of Use: Valid on all scheduled (timetable) services except cross-Channel and North Sea ferry trains.

Cost: 7 days - 1st class Adult £320/child £211, 2nd class £200/£132; 14 days - 1st class £500/£330, 2nd class £320/£211.20.

Purchase: From most staffed British Rail stations and from BT travel centres.

National Express

National Express offer a nationwide motor coach service in England and Wales and in Scotland where the service is operated in conjunction with Caledonian Express. The passes which it offers are the Tourist Trail Pass and Britexpress Card.

Tourist Trail Pass

Available to overseas visitors to Britain for unlimited travel on all the company's services for periods of 5, 8, 15, 22 or 30 consecutive days.

Cost:	Adult	Concession*
5 days	£56	£38
8 days	£78	£52
15 days	£116	£77
22 days	£138	£92
30 days	£160	£107

* *Concession rates apply to children and young people up to the age of 23, students of any age in full-time education and senior citizens not resident in the UK who are over the age of 60; proof of age and overseas residency will be required.*

Britexpress Card

Offers to overseas visitors to the UK an approximate 30% discount on all adult National Express and Caledonian Express standard fares for any consecutive 30-day period. First journey must be made within six months of purchase of the card.

Cost: Adult £12; children aged 5 to 15 automatically qualify for this discount. Young persons aged 16 to 23, students of any age with proof of full-time education and senior citizens aged 60 or over can buy a Discount Coach Card in the UK (cost £5) which gives the same discount on travel and is valid for one year.

Purchase: Both types of pass may be purchased outside the UK from National Express sales agents in Australia (Thomas Cook), Belgium, Brazil, Canada, Denmark, France, Germany, Greece, Hong Kong, India, Israel, Malta, Netherlands, New Zealand, Singapore, Spain, South Africa, the USA and Zimbabwe. In the UK: in London from Eurolines/National Express at 52 Grosvenor Gardens, from Victoria Coach Station, from the Tourist Information Centre at Victoria Railway Station, from the National Express Coach Travel Centre in Regent Street and from Golders Green Bus Station. At Heathrow Airport from the Coach Travel Centre at Central Bus Station and at Gatwick Airport from the National Express Coach Station or the Green Line Desk at the South Terminal. From National Express sales offices or appointed agents in Birmingham, Bournemouth*, Cambridge*, Chester*, Dover, Edinburgh, Exeter*, Glasgow, Leeds*, Manchester & Manchester Airport, Oxford, Portsmouth*, Southampton*, Stratford-upon-Avon and York plus a number of other agents in towns throughout Britain.
* *These points sell Britexpress Cards only.* Proof of residency outside the UK (passport, identity card, etc.) is required for all overseas visitors purchasing passes/cards in the UK.

BritRail & BritRail Flexi Passes, British Rail All Line Rovers, National Express Tourist Trail Passes & Britexpress Cards can all be used in England, Scotland & Wales. The section for the United Kingdom is now divided into countries - ENGLAND, NORTHERN IRELAND, SCOTLAND AND WALES - and under each country examples of all types of public transport passes are given, including some city and regional reduced-rate tickets,

ENGLAND (including Isle of Man & Jersey)

Rail Rovers and other reduced-rate rail tickets

Availability: Regional rail rovers are available to anyone for standard class travel on BR services.

Coverage: Gives 7 days unlimited travel in a designated area with a map of the region supplied.

Restrictions/Conditions of Use: Not available on excursion trains or Channel/North Sea ferries trains and (in some cases) before 0830 or 0900 Mondays to Fridays; further local restrictions on some regional tickets.

Cost (Adult): Freedom of the East Midlands £39.50; Freedom of the North West ££39.50; Freedom of the South West £45; Heart of England £39.50; Coast & Peaks (extends into Wales) ££39.50; Freedom of the North East £52;

Freedom of East Anglia £29.50; Devon* £30, Cornwall* £30, Severn/Avon/Wessex* £30. Approx. one-third reduction for children aged 5 to 15.
On these tickets, a second child travels free.

Purchase: Regional rover tickets are sold at main BR stations and travel centres in the area of the ticket and from appointed sales outlets; stations outside the area can often obtain the ticket but usually require seven days' notice.

Many 1, 2, 3 & 4-day tickets are available throughout England and whilst it is not possible to list all these a broad selection is given as follows:
Any 4 days out of an 8-day validity: North East Rover £38; North Country Flexi Rover £38; *Any 3 days out of a 7-day validity:* Severn/Avon/Wessex £22; Cornwall £19; Devon £22; Heart of England £29.50; East Midlands £29.50; North West £29.50; Coast & Peaks £29.50; East Anglia £19.50
Day Rovers and Day Rangers
Can be purchased in all regions of British Rail with the following being quoted as samples:
Anglia Day Ranger £11 - children two-thirds discount; Cumbrian Ranger £12; Tees £8.20; Tyne Valley £11.30; Settle Carlisle £12. There are a number of "Round Robin" tickets available for journeys on the Settle-Carlisle railway, the cost depending on which area the journey starts - Northern £15, North-West £21, London £34, West Midlands £25, some tickets being valid only on specified trains to and from Carlisle and all tickets valid Mondays to Thursdays and Satur-days (Not Sats. in July and August). Some one-day tickets are available for the summer months only. On lines where there are unstaffed stations, some day rangers can be bought from the guard on the train. Other area tickets which com-bine local rail, bus, ferry and Metro/Underground railway services are shown separately.
Network SouthEast issue a Network Card valid for one year which offers up to one-third discount on travel within the South East region; it can be shared by a second named holder and can be used by up to three other adults travelling together and up to 4 children (aged 5-15) who pay a flat rate of £1 each. *Cost:* £12 for sole use, £15 for joint use; £8 sole use and £10 joint use for senior citizens and holders of Young Persons Railcards.

London Travelcards *U*

Availability: Available to anyone for travel by public transport in the Greater London area.

Coverage: Gives unlimited travel on London's Network SouthEast trains, most London Regional Transport and some Green Line buses (not Airbus services), Underground railway network and the Docklands Light Railway based on a 6-zone system of travel. One-day, weekly. monthly and annual travelcards are available and the cost depends of the number of zones for which the ticket is valid.

Restrictions/Conditions of Use: A passport-type photograph is required for the photocard - issued free of charge - which must accompany travelcards for 7 days or more; proof of age required for childrens' travelcards. One-day travelcards cannot be used before 0930 Mondays to Fridays or on night or excursion buses; if issued outside the Travelcard area one return journey to the Travelcard area is permitted.

Examples of Travelcard prices: One-day cards - two zone (Zones 1 & 2) £2.30, four zone £2.60, all zone card £2.90; flat rate for children (5-15) of £1. From Underground stations outside the zonal area - between £3.20 and £3.80.
Weekly cards - Zone 1 £7.80, Zones 1 & 2 £10, Zones 1, 2 & 3 £13.80, all zones £22. Monthly cards - Zone 1 £30, Zones 1 & 2 £38.40, Zones 1, 2 & 3 £53, all zones £84.50

Purchase: One-day cards can be purchased from Underground railway station ticket offices and self-service machines and from appointed newsagents throughout the London area. All other types of ticket can be bought from Underground and Network SouthEast station and a limited range are also sold by newsagents.

Outside the United Kingdom a *London Visitor Travelcard* can be bought from authorised agents and gives a similar coverage to that of London Travelcards; the cost is 3 days - Adult US$18/child (5-15) US$8, 4 days US$23/US$10, 7 daysUS$40/US$16. Also available is the *London Extra Pass* which is comparable to the Network SouthEast Card and costs 1st class US$95 Adult/Standard Class US$75 for 3 days; 1st class US$120/Standard US$90 for 4 days and 1st class US$170/Standard US$135 for 7 days. Children half price. Available from British Rail sales agents worldwide.

Isle of Man Rover Tickets

Offering unlimited travel on the railways and buses of the Isle of Man
Rail Rover
Valid for any 3 days travel within 7 during the period March 29-Sept. 28 between Douglas and Port Erin by Steam Railway and between Douglas and Ramsey by Manx Electric Railway and including one return trip by Snaefell Mountain Railway.
Cost: Adult £9.90, child aged 5 to 15 half price. Families purchasing two adult and two child tickets, third and fourth children travel free.
May be purchased from all rail and bus stations and sales offices on the Isle of Man as well as authorised hotels and information centres. By post from Isle of Man Transport (details on the inside front cover of this guidebook). 1-day rovers are also available.
Bus Rovers
Unrestricted travel on the Isle of Man bus network, valid for one day or any 3 days out of 7.
Cost: 1-day Adult £3.90; any 3 from 7 days £7.50
All other details as for the Rail Rover.
Rail/Bus Ticket
Unrestricted travel on all bus, steam train, electric tram, mountain railway and horse tram services for 7 consecutive days.
Cost: £17.95 adult.
All other details as for the Rail Rover.

Isle of Wight Rover Tickets

Unlimited travel by British Rail trains (Ryde-Shanklin) and Southern Vectis/Seaview Services buses on the Isle of Wight for 1, 7 or 28 days; also includes "Places of Interest" discount scheme.

Cost (Summer prices): 1 day £5.45, 7 days £18.45, 28 days £35; children aged 5 to 13 approx. half price.

Tickets may be purchased from Southern Vectis travel offices, tourist information centres and Isle of Wight BR stations; one and seven day tickets can be bought on boarding buses.

Jersey Explorer Tickets 🚌

"Explore Jersey" bus passes are available to anyone for unlimited travel on Jersey Motor Transport scheduled bus services throughout the island.

Cost: 1-day pass £2.60, 3 days £6.50, 7 days £11.50. Child reduction (for children aged 3 to 15) applies only to the 7-day pass which costs £6.50

Passes can be bought from the Weighbridge Bus Station near the harbour at St.Helier.

Tyne & Wear *U*

In the Tyne & Wear region, Network Ticketing (NTL) have a wide range of Traveltickets and a Day Rover available for unlimited use on local buses, the Metro system, Shields Ferry and the BR service between Sunderland and Newcastle. Prices of Traveltickets depend on the number of zones required for travel.

Sample prices: A one-day Rover (scratch-and-ride variety) costs £2.50. Other Network Traveltickets range from one-week tickets at £6.30 for 2 zones and £9 for all zones to four-week tickets at £22.10 for 2 zones and £31.50 for all zones. There are also Off-Peak Traveltickets. A Travelcard requiring a colour photo and costing £1 must be purchased at the same time as a Travelticket.

Most local bus operators accept Traveltickets on their services and the tickets can be purchased from their travelcentres displaying the "Network Traveltickets" sign and from a number of Metro and railway stations. The Day Rover is available from a number of sales outlets and in advance by post from NTL at Gallowgate, Newcastle upon Tyne.

Tyne & Wear PTE operate Tyne & Wear Metro rail network, the Shields ferries and a number of local bus services in the Newcastle area. They offer one-day Explorer tickets - Adult £4.10, children £1.70, family £7.50, senior citizen £3.10 which can be bought at Travelcentres and on some buses.

West Midlands 🚌 🚋

West Midlands Travel issue a variety of reduced-rate tickets for their bus services with some tickets including rail travel on BR lines in the West Midlands (Centro) PTE region.

Cost: A Daybus ticket costs £1.60 adult and £3.20 family; a Daytripper covering West Midlands bus and rail travel costs £2.10 adult and £3.65 family; a Midline Day Ranger on BR's Midline Network is £1.80 adult & £3.15 family in the Centro area and £5 adult & £10 family in the whole Midline area. Children at half price; family tickets cover 2 adults and up to 4 children. Monday to Friday early morning travel restrictions apply to one-day tickets. There are one-week Regional Travelcards costing £8.25 for bus travel and £10.40 for combined bus and rail travel (West Midlands County only) and Railmaster Tickets for train journeys in West Midlands County area cost £8 per week and £26.50 for four weeks. Also available are four-week Regional Travelcards, one and four week Area Travelcards (for travel in Coventry, Walsall/Cannock & Wolverhampton districts), Off-Peak Travelcards and Young Persons Travelcards.

Daybus tickets can be purchased on buses and from local post offices; rail and combined bus/rail tickets are available at railway stations in the Midline Network or Midlands County areas and all reduced-rate tickets are sold at West Midland Travel shops, at authorised agents and at the Centro Enquiry at Birmingham New Street Station. Photographs are required for passes other than one-day tickets.

Metro (West Yorkshire)

West Yorkshire PTE issue Metro Day-Rovers and MetroPasses for unlimited travel on their bus and rail network. The DayRovers are not valid for travel before 0930 Mondays to Fridays. The MetroPass is a transferable weekly ticket which can be used by anyone (regardless of who purchased it) at any time.

Cost: DayRover - Adult £1.40, children (aged 5-13) half price; Family DayRover* £2.80; Metropass £8.90 for 7 consecutive days.

* *Consisting of 2 adults and up to 3 children or 1 adult and up to 4 children.*

West Yorkshire PTE also offer weekly and monthly MetroCards and Metro SaverStrip (12-ride) tickets.

Tickets are sold at main railway stations in the region, Metro Saver Centres, bus stations, post offices and a large number of shops.

Other Regional Reduced-Rate Travel Tickets

Greater Manchester PTE

Weekly and monthly Saver tickets for bus and combined bus & rail travel including a weekly adult bus pass at £11.25 and for young people (aged 16-19) costing £7.85. A Wayfarer day runabout ticket valid on buses and trains costs £4.50

Merseytravel

Saveaway day tickets and other zoned tickets give opportunity for travel in 1, 2, 4 or 5 zones. An All Zones ticket extends from Liverpool to Birkenhead, Wallasey and the Wirral, Southport and St. Helens. A Saveaway day ticket for all zones costs £2.75 and "Across-Mersey" ticket £2.30. There are also off-peak, weekly and monthly zone tickets with reduced fares for young people.

South Yorkshire PTE

Travelmaster Countrywide Travel Passes give unlimited travel on all bus and local rail services within South Yorkshire, a weekly pass costing £9.75 and monthly £35.50. There is also a monthly Railmaster ticket.

Derbyshire Wayfarer

Valid for travel on all scheduled bus and rail routes in Derbyshire and extending outside the county to Sheffield, Macclesfield, Uttoxeter and Burton-on-Trent; also offers discounts at a number of tourist attractions. Costs £6 adult; half price children.

Ribble

The Ribble Country Explorer ticket is valid on a number of bus routes in Lancashire as well as Ribble services in Greater Manchester, Merseyside and North Yorkshire, Cumberland local bus services and all Hyndburn Transport buses. Daily tickets cost £3.60 adult, £2.40 child and £9.50 family; weekly tickets at £16 adult, £10.50 child and £38 family. Special rates for senior citizens.

Blackpool Transport

Travelcards are valid on all scheduled bus

routes of Blackpool Transport Services Ltd. and services of Blackpool & Fleetwood Tramway, 1-day cards being available on buses and trams. 1-day Travelcards cost £3, 3-day £7 and 7-day £10

East Yorkshire

East Yorkshire Motor Services Ltd. offer Explorer Tickets for their own and Scarborough and District bus services for one day's travel. Adult price is £3.80, family £7.69 with usual reductions for children and senior citizens.

Eastern National

and Thamesway bus services provide an Essex Ranger scratch-and-ride day ticket on their services with adult (£5.25), family (£10.50), child & senior citizen (£4) fares. Also available are ChelmerCards for travel in the Chelmsford district and Colchester Travelcards.

NORTHERN IRELAND

Emerald Card

Availability: Available to anyone for unlimited travel on the services of Northern Ireland Railways (NIR), Ulsterbus (normal scheduled routes and Belfast Citybus services), Irish Rail, Bus Eireann and Dublin Bus.

Coverage: Permits 8 days travel out of a specified period of 15 days or 15 days out of 30.

Cost: 8 days in 15 - Sterling £95/IR£100; 15 days in 30 - £161/IR£170. Children aged 3 to 15 half price.
Prices in pounds sterling and Irish punts are subject to a fluctuating exchange rate.

Purchase: May be obtained from principal stations and depots of Northern Ireland Railways, Irish Rail, Bus Eireann and Ulsterbus. Proof of age may be required when purchasing a child card.

Irish Rover

Irish Rail and Northern Ireland Railways issue two types of joint rover ticket valid only on their rail services and purchased from their principal stations and travel sales offices in Northern Ireland and the Irish Republic.
Cost: 8 days out of 15 days (valid April to October) £55; 15 days out of 30 (valid all year) £80

Northern Ireland Rail Runabout

Available to anyone for 7 consecutive days of unlimited travel by standard class on all NIR scheduled services (also to Dundalk) between April and October.
Cost: £27.50; half price for children aged 5 to 15.
Sold by principal stations and travel offices of Northern Ireland Railways.

Freedom of Northern Ireland

Issued by Ulsterbus and valid for unlimited travel on Ulsterbus and Belfast Citybus scheduled services in Northern Ireland.
Cost: 1-day - adult £8; 7-day - adult £20.
Concession fares for children aged 3 to 16 and senior citizens over 65 are half the adult fare.
Purchased from Ulsterbus depots and from their office at 10 Glengall Street in Belfast.

Freedom of Scotland Rover

Availability: Available to anyone for unlimited travel on British Rail scheduled train services in Scotland.

Coverage: Valid for 7 or 15 days in standard class for services north of Carlisle and Berwick-on-Tweed. Also available are FlexiRovers for any 4 days travel out of a specified 8-day validity and 10 days out of a 15-day period.

Restrictions/Conditions of Use: Not valid on steam services between Fort William and Mallaig and v.v. The 4 out of 8 days ticket cannot be used on services arriving at Aberdeen, Inverness, Edinburgh Haymarket or Glasgow before 0915 Mondays to Fridays.

Cost: 15 days (Gold Ticket) £97; 7 days (Silver Ticket) £64. FlexiRovers: Any 4 days out of 8 - £48; any 10 days out of 15 - £88. Approx. one-third discount for children aged 5 to 15.

Heart of Scotland Rover

Same conditions and facilities as the Freedom of Scotland Rover but valid for 7 days on BR lines between Perth and:
Aviemore, Aberdeen, Edinburgh and Stirling.
Not valid before 0800 Mondays to Fridays.
Cost: £37

Festival Cities Rover

Valid for 3 days travel out of a specified period of 7 days for standard class BR journeys between Edinburgh and:

North Berwick, Stirling, Glasgow Queen Street via Falkirk, Glasgow Central via Shotts, Cowdenbeath and Kirkcaldy.
On Mondays to Fridays not valid for travel before 0915 or for joining Glasgow-Edinburgh (and v.v.) trains between 1625 and 1740.
Cost: £16.50

North Highland Rover

Same conditions and facilities as the Freedom of Scotland Rover except that it is valid for 7 days on BR lines between Inverness and:
Kyle of Lochalsh, Wick & Thurso, Aberdeen and Aviemore. Not valid Mondays to Fridays on trains arriving at Aberdeen or Inverness before 0900.
Cost: £35

West Highland Rover

Same conditions and facilities as the Freedom of Scotland Rover but valid for 7 days and available on BR lines Fort William-Mallaig, Fort William-Glasgow and Crianlarich-Oban. Not valid on Fort William-Mallaig steam services.
Cost: £35 (Price expected to decrease to £32 from Sept. 29)

Purchase of all Rover tickets in Scotland: Rover tickets are sold at main British Rail stations and travel centres in the area of the ticket and from appointed sales agents. Stations outside the area can usually obtain tickets but often require seven days notice.

Highlands & Islands Travelpass

Availability: Available to anyone for 7 or 13 days unlimited standard class travel by

British Rail scheduled services in north and west Scotland plus some ferry services.

Coverage: Valid for travel within the Highlands and Islands by Scotrail services, Caledonian MacBrayne's Western Isles ferries and P & O Ferries Orkney service between Scrabster and Stromness. Also offers a one-third discount on standard bus fares on main bus routes in the srea including those of Scottish Citylink Coaches, Highland/Midland/Western Scottish Omnibuses, Caledonian Express, Gaelic Buses (West Highland Services), Rapsons Coaches, Skye-Ways Express Coach Services, D. MacLennan, West Highland Motor Services (Mallaig & Fort William), Henderson Hiring and on Post Bus services. Further benefits are a return rail or bus ticket from Glasgow, Edinburgh or Aberdeen to destinations in the Highlands and Islands area and the issue of a Scotpass entitling the holder to discounts at a variety of shops, hotels, restaurants and tourist attractions in the area and in Glasgow, Edinburgh and Aberdeen.

Cost: Peak period (June to September) - 7 days over an 8-day period £65, 13 days over a 15-day period £90. Off-peak period (remainder of the year) - 7/8 days £40 and 13/15 days £60.

Purchase: By post from Highland Direct, Dingwall IV15 9JE, Scotland (☎ 0349-65000). Obtainable from main BR stations and travel centres and Scottish bus companies' offices in Scotland, from the Caledonian MacBrayne Ferry Terminal at Gourock and a number of Highlands and Islands Tourism information centres; in London from Euston, Kings Cross and Victoria railway stations, from Scottish Citylink Coaches and the British Travel Centre (both in Regent Street) and from the Scottish Centre in Cockspur Street. Overseas the pass can be purchased from Scots American Travel Advisors at Harrington Park, New Jersey and from British Rail International in Basel and Milan but must then be validated by one of the following offices: BR Waverley Edinburgh, Central & Queen Street stations in Glasgow, The Enquiry Office at Inverness and the Travel Centres at St. Andrew Square Bus Station in Edinburgh and the Buchanan Street Bus Station in Glasgow.

Explorer Ticket (Scottish Citylink) 🚌

Valid for 7 days unlimited travel on Scottish Citylink motor coaches and "Summerlink" services on mainland Scotland and the Isle of Skye. Also offers 20% reduction on an adult period return coach fare on one of their Anglo-Scottish services.

Cost: High Season (May to September) - Adult £40, child (aged 5 to 15) and young person* £30. Reduced fares for the low season (remainder of the year) of £32 adult and £24 child/young person*.

* Available to young people who hold a "Young Scot" card or an equivalent type of card in any other country.

Can be bought from Scottish Citylink Coaches in Glasgow and Edinburgh and from appointed Scottish Citylink sales agents throughout the UK. Photo is necessary at time of purchase.

Strathclyde Transport *U*

Centred on Glasgow, Strathclyde Transport produce a number of reduced-rate tickets for travel on their bus, local rail and Underground railway systems. A Scratch-and-Ride Family Day Tripper covers all Strathclyde scheduled services and extends to Loch Lomond, the Clyde coast, Ayr and Girvan. On the Glasgow Underground there are one-day Heritage Trail Tickets whilst 7-day and 28-tickets are also available; the seven and twenty-eight day tickets nesessitate a passport-size photograph for a free Photocard issued by the Transcentre at St. Enoch Station.

One-day tickets cannot be used before 0900 Mondays to Fridays.

Cost: Family Day Tripper costs £10 for 2 adults and up to 4 children and £5.50 for 1 adult and up to 2 children. One-day Heritage Trail tickets cost £1.60, 7-day tickets £4.50 and 28-days £16.

All tickets are sold by Strathclyde Transport Travel Centre at St. Enoch Square at St. Enoch Square, Glasgow (☎ 041-226 4826) and Family Day Trippers from staffed ScotRail stations in Strathclyde, St. Enoch Station Transcentre, from appointed sales agents and from sales outlets of the participating bus operators.

Lothian Region Transport

Lothian Region Transport (LRT) have a Touristcard facility for visitors to Edinburgh which offers unlimited travel on LRT city bus services (not valid on Airlink Coach Service 100) for between 2 and 13 days and also gives reductions on their coach tours. In addition LRT sell 1-week and 4-week Ridacards and one-day Freedom Tickets.

Cost: 2 days - Adult £4.20, child (aged 5-15) £3.10; 3 days - adult £5.30, child £3.90. Prices then increase by £1.10 per

day per adult and £0.80 per day per child to 13-days fares of £16.30 Adult and £11.90 child. A 1-day Freedom Ticket costs £1.50 Adult and £1 child.

Sold by LRT's head office at 14 Queen Street and by the Ticket Centre at Waverley Bridge.

Bluebird Northern

Bluebird Northern - part of Northern Scottish Omnibuses offer a one-day Bluebird Rover Ticket for all their services throughout the Grampian Region which includes Royal Deeside, Speyside, Elgin and the Moray Coast as well as the city of Aberdeen.

Cost: £6.50 Adult, £3.25 children and senior citizens.

Purchased on board bus.

Island Runabout Tickets

Caledonian MacBrayne issue two types of 'Island Runabout' tickets valid for 8 or 15 consecutive days or for three months for foot passengers or passengers with vehicles on most of their ferry services in Scotland.

Island Hopscotch fares are valid for three months and cover 24 pre-planned combinations of routes with prices - per person - ranging from £3.20 to £27.15 and with appropriate accompanying charges for vehicles.

Island Rover tickets cost £30 per person for 8 days and £44 for 15 days with appropriate vehicles charges based on overall length.

Tickets can be purchased from Caledonian MacBrayne at the Ferry Terminal, Gourock PA19 1QP (☎ 0475-34531) and Island Rover tickets from Caledonian MacBrayne major terminals on the mainland or from the purser on the Gourock-

Dunoon, Wemyss Bay-Rothesay, Ardrossan-Brodick or Oban-Craignure ferries.

Scottish Highland Rover Airpass (British Airways) ✈

Availability: Available to anyone for travel on British Airway's Highlands and Islands services.

Coverage: Valid for up to 8 flights on British Airways routes between Glasgow/Edinburgh-Aberdeen-Wick-Orkney and Shetland Islands, Glasgow-Inverness-Orkney & Shetland, Glasgow-Benbecula & Stornoway, Inverness-Stornoway. Minimum period of travel is 8 days and maximum 21 days.

Restrictions/Conditions of Use: Ticket must be purchased at least 7 days before commencing first journey. Only one return trip is allowed between any pair of destinations. The pass is not available for local travel between Wick and Orkney.

Cost: £196

Purchase: From British Airways Shops or from appointed agents.

WALES

Rail Rovers 🚋
Freedom of Wales
Availability: Available to anyone for unlimited travel in standard class on British Rail scheduled services in Wales.

Coverage: Valid for 7 days as per the above conditions plus journeys between Shotton and Chester, Crewe and Chester and Crewe-Shrewsbury-Hereford-Abergavenny.

Cost: £45
North & Mid Wales
Valid for 7 days standard class travel on BR lines in Wales bounded by and including Aberystwyth, Shrewsbury, Crewe and Holyhead. Also valid on Crosville and associated bus services in Gwynedd and on the Ffestiniog Railway.
Cost: £30

Coast & Peaks (North Wales)
Valid for 7 days or any 3 days out of 7 days in standard class travel on BR lines from Liverpool, Manchester & Derby westward to New Brighton and Holyhead and to Blaenau Ffestiniog; southward to Church Stretton.
Cost: 7 days - £39.50; 3 days out of 7 - £29.50.

Purchase: The three previous Rover tickets can be purchased at main British Rail stations and travel centres in the srea of the ticket and from appointed sales outlets. Stations outside the area can often obtain tickets but usually require seven days notice.

A Heart of Wales Rambler is valid between May and September for weekday tickets and July-Sept. for Sunday tickets on the Shrewsbury-Swansea line for one day (Mondays to Saturdays) at £7 adult; Sunday tickets cost £5 adult (with children aged 5 to 15 half price) and £10 family.
Also in Wales there are a number of day Rambler and Ranger tickets, an example being the Cardiff Valleys Day Ranger costing £4.20 (price subject to increase).

Great Little Trains Wanderer Ticket 🚂

Available to anyone for 4 or 8 days unlimited travel on the Bala Lake, Brecon Mountain, Ffestiniog, Llanberis Lake, Talyllyn, Vale of Rheidol, Welsh Highland and Welshpool & Llanfair narrow gauge railways. The tickets are valid from March 25 to October 31.

Cost: 4 days £18, 8 days £25, children aged 5 to 15 at half price.

May be obtained from the principal stations of the participating railways and by post from GLTW, Pant Station, Dowlais, Merthyr Tydfil, Mid Glamorgan CF48 2UP.

Crosville Wanderer Tickets 🚌

Crosville bus services covering the whole of North Wales including the Snowdonia National Park and the Cambrian Coast offer one-day Wanderer tickets at £4.50 which can be purchased on board bus and weekly tickets at £9.25 (no child reductions) sold by Crosville depots and main post offices in the area. Not valid on the Traws Cambria Bangor-Cardiff route 700.

USA

USA Rail Passes 🚂

Availability: Available to permanent residents of countries outside the United States and Canada for rail travel within the USA.

Coverage: Valid for 45 days in unrestricted coach class travel with unlimited stopovers on a national or regional basis on the National Railroad Passenger Corporation (Amtrak) network in the USA and - for the National and Eastern Region passes - to Montréal and Niagara Falls in Canada.

Restrictions/Conditions of Use: Not valid on trains of other operators or on Boston suburban trains of Amtrak. Supplement payable on Metroliner services. Travel tickets are issued on presentation of the pass.

Cost: **Nationwide (Entire Amtrak System) -** US$299
Regional Passes: Eastern Region - US$179; Western Region - US$229; Far Western - US$179; Florida - US$69.

50% reduction for children aged 2 to 11. Prices in sterling and other currencies depend on the varying US dollar exchange rate.

Purchase: From Amtrak appointed agents in over 50 countries worldwide including Thomas Cook in the UK **(via Compass - details at foot of page three).** Passport must be presented at time of purchase. Not normally purchasable in the USA but sold in Puerto Rico, the American Virgin Islands and Guam.

Greyhound Lines Ameripass

Availability: Available to anyone resident outside North America (including part of Mexico) for bus travel nationwide in the USA.

Coverage: Offers unlimited bus (motor coach) travel for 7, 15 or 30 consecutive days on Greyhound and Trailways bus lines and on other participating carriers' services. There is also a special 4-day midweek ticket valid Monday to Thursday.

Restrictions/Conditions of Use: The Ameripass is not valid for travel in Canada except on the Greyhound routes Seattle-Vancouver, Fargo-Winnipeg and Boston/New York-Montréal. Side-trips between Las Vegas and Hoover Dam/Death Valley are not covered in the fares. Validity commences the first time the pass is used; stopovers are allowed.

Cost: 7 days - £75, 15 days - £120, 30 days £150. Midweek 4-day ticket £45. Daily extensions - which must be purchased at the same time as the pass - cost £10 per day. There is an additional charge of US$12.90 per person for the round trip Flagstaff, Arizona to the Grand Canyon.

Purchase: May be purchased in the UK from Greyhound World Travel in East Grinstead, Sussex and from Thomas Cook **(via Compass - details at foot of page three).** Worldwide from Greyhound sales agents outside North America.

City Transportation Passes   *U*

Some American cities offer reduced-rate travel tickets suitable for overseas visitors. We list a selection of these passes below: The *"Boston Passport"* visitors runabout pass gives 3 or 7 days unlimited travel on all Rapid Transit Lines and local bus services of Massachusetts Bay Transportation Authority and costs (1990 prices) US$8 for 3 days and US$16 for 7 days and if purchased after 1500 hours on the first valid day, an extra day's cover is added; additional benefits include discounts at restaurants, museums and places of interest. San Francisco Municipal Railway offer a *Muni "Passport"* for a day at US$6 and for 3 days at US$10 which affords unlimited travel on their vehicles - including cable cars - as well as a variety of discounts. Washington Metropolitan Area Transit Authority issue a *Family/ Tourist Pass* suitable for families or groups of four persons with 4 passes costing US$6 and allowing one day's travel at weekends and Federal holidays on their Metrobus and Metrorail services. The Metropolitan Transit Development Board of San Diego have available a *One-Day Tripper* at US$4 and a *Four-Day Tripper* at US$12 permitting unlimited travel on all regular bus routes, Trolley and San Diego Bay Ferry services. Portland Tri-Met issue a day ticket.

Visa Passes (Northwest Airlines) ✈

Availability: Available only to persons residing outside the USA for travel on Northwest Airlines and Northwest Airlink services within Continental (Mainland) USA.

Restrictions/Conditions of Use: Passes can only be used in conjunction with Roundtrip International travel on the scheduled services of Northwest. Proof of country of residence and Roundtrip International travel must be produced on request. Stopovers are permitted but no more than two may be made at any one point. Travel must be completed within 60 days of first flight date or within 120 days after arrival in the USA, whichever occurs first. One flight coupon must be surrendered for each flight boarded; minimum of 4 coupons. Supplementary coupons are available for travel to Hawaii, Alaska, Mexico and the Caribbean. Minimum stay of 7 days in the USA for the Visit USA Pass.

The 60 Day Confirmed Seat Pass costs US$399 adult and US$359 child in economy class with additional coupons at US$35 each and in first class US$649 with additional coupons at US$50 each; no child fare in 1st class.

The 60 Day Visit USA Airpass costs £188 per 2 coupons with additional coupons at £59; no child fares.

Northwest also offer Open Passes in economy and first class and 30-day Standby Passes.

All prices are subject to alteration.

Available from Northwest Airlines sales offices and their agents outside North America.

Air Passes (Continental Airlines) ✈

Availability: Available to visitors to the USA by Transatlantic or Transpacific routes of Continental Airlines and valid for Continental (Mainland) USA services of Continental Airlines in economy class.

Restrictions/Conditions of Use: Cost is per coupon with a minimum of 3 and maximum of 10 and additional fares can be added on for journeys to the Caribbean, Hawaii and Mexico. All travel must be completed within 60 days of first flight or within 120 days after arrival in the USA, whichever occurs first.

Cost: 3 coupons cost US$267 adult/ US$207 child rising to US$589 adult/ US$529 child for 10 coupons. Prices liable to alteration.

Purchase: From Continental sales offices outside North America and authorised agents worldwide.

Visit USA Passes (America West Airlines) ✈

Availability: America West offer Nationwide and Tristate Passes which must be purchsed before arrival in the USA and with prices per flight.

Restrictions/Conditions of Use: Tickets are valid for 60 days from date of first flight which must be booked before arrival in the USA. Flights on America West services in Continental (Mainland) USA allow only one round trip.

The Nationwide Pass (minimum purchase four flights and maximum twelve) covers the whole America West system with the exception of Calgary and Edmonton in Canada, Honolulu, Steamboat Springs and Vail, special add-on fares being available for these destinations.

Cost: £40 per flight with additional flights over four costing £30 per flight; children aged under 11 are charged £32 and £23 respectively.

Tristate Passes (minimum purchase two flight and maximum ten) are valid only in the states of California, Arizona and Nevada with special add on fares applying as for the Nationwide Pass.

Cost: £30 per flight with additional flights over two costing £25 per flight; children aged under 11 £25 and £20 per flight respectively.

Purchase: From America West sales offices outside North America and from appointed agents worldwide.

Other reduced-rate air travel fares within the USA include "Visit USA" (VUSA) fares offered by USAir and American Airlines, Hawaiian Airlines "Visit Hawaii USA Fare", "Islands in the Sky", "Hawaiian Island Specials", "Visit Six Islands" and "Inter-Island" fares and Delta Airlines' "Discover America Fares". Delta Airlines also have a 30-day Standby Air Pass at US$449 and a 60-day Air Pass at US$749 USAir offer Senior Saver fares.

Thomas Cook European Timetable

The Thomas Cook European Timetable, first published in 1873 and popular for many years as the Continental Timetable, covers rail services throughout Europe including Britain, Ireland and Eastern Europe with timings for nearly 50,000 trains. Plus detailed information on cross-Channel and North Sea ferry services, shipping services in the Baltic and Mediterranean, quick reference index maps and city plans.

The timetable is published and updated monthly; advance timings for international trains appear in special summer and winter supplements all contained in the timetable.

Thomas Cook Rail Map of Europe

The popular Thomas Cook Rail Map of Europe, published every 2 years, is a three-colour map in approximately 1:5 000 000 scale, 860 x 685mm, showing passenger lines throughout Europe from the Atlantic coast to Moscow and the Black Sea and in countries bordering the Mediterranean. A number of enlargements on the reverse side give added details for central Europe, the Rhine-Rühr district and a number of major cities. Separate symbols are used for main and secondary lines, electrified lines, narrow gauge and mountain lines, scenic routes, railways under construction and train ferries, with bilingual English/French legend.

Thomas Cook World Rail Map

Companion map to the Thomas Cook Overseas Timetable, the World Rail Map covers 150 rail systems in 88 countries and six continents and includes all major freight lines. Colour coded rail networks with gauge information in panels.

Double sided with enlarged maps of India, North America and Japan on the reverse side; size 1150 x 530mm, folding to 230 x 130mm.

Thomas Cook Overseas Timetable

Thomes Cook publish a timetable six times per year to show the principal surface travel facilities for most countries outside Europe; normally published in the first week of January, March, May, July, September and November. Ideal for travellers making intercontinental journeys by air who then require surface connections in the country of destination and for travel agents with clients travelling outside Europe.

Principal Eurail Sales Agents

Not all of the following agents are issuing offices for Eurail tickets and therefore may not be able to issue them without prior notice.

The list is subject to amendment.

ARGENTINA - From RENFE (Spanish National Railways) and CIT in Buenos Aires.

AUSTRALIA - Thomas Cook in major cities; also from CIT Australia, National Australia Bank Travel Service and Concorde International Travel.

BAHRAIN - Manama

BOLIVIA - La Paz

BRAZIL - From Wagons-Lits Turismo in a number of cities and CIT in São Paulo and Porto Alegre

CANADA - From French National Railroads in Montréal, Toronto and Vancouver; also from CIT Tours Corporation and DER Travel Service (DB-German Federal Railroad) and from their appointed agents throughout Canada.

CHILE - Santiago de Chile and Valparaiso.

COLOMBIA - Bogota, Cali and Medellin.

COSTA RICA - San Jose

ECUADOR - Quito

EGYPT - From Thomas Cook in Cairo.

HONG KONG - From Thomas Cook, Lufthansa German Airlines, Hong Kong Student Travel Bureau and Schenker Travel.

INDIA - Bangalore, Bombay, Calcutta, Madras and New Delhi.

INDONESIA - Jakarta.

ISRAEL - Haifa, Jerusalem and Tel Aviv.

JAPAN - Tokyo, Fukuoka, Kobe, Kyoto, Nagoya, Osaka, Sapporo and Sendai and from JTB branches throughout Japan.

KOREA (South) - Seoul and Pusan.

MALAYSIA - Kuala Lumpur.

MEXICO - From Wagons-Lits Mexicana, Viajes Kuoni and Viajes Melia in Mexico City, from Wagons-Lits offices in Guadalajara, Merida and Monterrey and from Destinos Mundiales in Guadalajara.

NEW ZEALAND - From Thomas Cook and Atlantic & Pacific Agencies in Auckland.

PAKISTAN - Karachi.

PARAGUAY - Asunción.

PERU - Lima.

PHILIPPINES - Metro Manila (Makati).

PUERTO RICO - San Juan (Santurce).

SAUDI ARABIA - Jeddah and Riyadh.

SINGAPORE - Thomas Cook and American Express.

SOUTH AFRICA - Cape Town.

SRI LANKA - Colombo.

TAIWAN - Taipei.

THAILAND - Bangkok.

UNITED ARAB EMIRATES - From Thomas Cook in Abu Dhabi and Deira-Dubai.

U.S.A. - From French National Railroads at White Plains, New York and from their sales offices and those of a number of appointed sales agents throughout the United States including Thomas Cook. Purchased by post from Forsyth Travel Library at the address given below.

URUGUAY - Montevideo.

VENEZUELA - Caracas.

The principal Eurail ticket sales outlets are in the above cities but there are many more in places in Australia, Canada, Japan and the USA.

The address of Forsyth Travel Library is 9154 West 57th Street, P.O. Box 2975, Shawnee Mission, KS 66201-1375. ☎ Toll Free 1-800-"FORSYTH" (1-800-367-7984); fax (913) 384-3553.